THE WORLDWIDE GUIDE TO CHEAP AIRFARES

THE WORLDWIDE GUIDE
TO CHEAP AIRFARES

How to Travel

The World

Without Breaking

The Bank

MICHAEL WM. McCOLL

INSIDER PUBLICATIONS

San Francisco

Project Management and Design: Lisa Schulz, Elysium Design
Editor: Katherine Poyma

Contributing Writers
Chris Farabee, Miami · Richard Heend, Hong Kong · Peter Cramer, Sydney

Researchers
Beth Baron (Chicago) · Chris Blunt (Hong Kong) · Marcus Colombano (Singapore) · Paul Eisenburg (New York) · Diane Groce (Bangkok) · Chris Linson (Bangkok) · Michele Tanenbaum (New York) · Allison Tollstam (Singapore) · Joris Wiggers (Tokyo)

Thanks to
American Express Travel Related Services · Ian Berry · David Binetti · Ken Blaschke · Baker & Taylor · Bookpeople · Dennis Brown · Dave & Rebecca Carrillo · Mel Cohen, Cut Throat Travel · Cathy Cutler · Byron Deeter · Patti Eger · Karel Fegyl · Tim Fishman · Donna Galassi, Foghorn Press · Peter Gill, Jupiter Air · Benjamin Goldsmith · Steven D. Grothe · Larry Habegger · Pat Houdek, OAG · Ingram Books · International Air Transport Association · Duane Johnson · Rachel Joplin · Byron Lutz, IAATC · L-S Books · Gill Meadows, Sanctuary (Kho Phangan, Thailand) · Doug Moshy · New Image Photo · Bill Newlin, Moon Travel Handbooks · Mark Nelson, OAG · Nolo Press · Allen Noren, GNN's Travelers' Center · George Ouzts, Travelxn.com · Pacific Pipeline · Andria Piekarz, STA Travel · Greg Posey, Council Travel · Quality Books · Takeyoshi Sakai · Bob Sanchez · Laura Sheppard, Easy Going · Ron Silverton · Sunbelt Publications · SF Net · Tourism Authority of Thailand · Topaz Enterprises · Upper Access Books · United States Department of Transportation · Ed Vaz, Jupiter Air · Jason Wallace · Jim Williams, *The Hostel Handbook*

Thanks for providing guidance and inspiration
Doug and Kathe McColl · Gert and Betty King

Eternal gratitude to the Project Team
Lisa and Kathy, whose professional skill, unflagging dedication and general brilliance made this book possible.

Some current courier and consolidator fares were provided courtesy of The International Association of Air Courier Travelers, PO Box 1349, Lake Worth, FL 33460. Telephone (407) 582 8320. Copyright © 1996 International Features. Benchmark full coach fares were provided courtesy of *The Official Airline Guides, Electronic Edition.*

Insider Publications, 2124 Kittredge Street, Third Floor, Berkeley, CA 94704 USA

Printing History:

June 1989	First Edition
December 1989	Second Edition
June 1990	Third Edition
December 1992	Fourth Edition
January 1995	Fifth Edition
July 1995	Fifth Edition, Second Printing
June 1996	Sixth Edition
March 1998	Sixth Edition, Second Printing

ISBN: 0-9633512-3-0, Library of Congress Catalog Card Number: 94-77556

♲ Printed in the United States of America on recycled paper.

CONTENTS

Vancouver
Seattle

San Francisco

Chicago

Toronto

Montreal

Boston

New York

Philadelphia

Kauai
Honolulu

Los Angeles

Maui

Orlando

Miami

Nassau

Puerto Vallarta
Mexico City

Cancún

San Juan

Santo Domingo

Kingston

St Johns

Guatemala
San Salvador

San Jose

Caracas

Port of Spain

Bogotá

Quito
Guayaquil

Lima

La Paz

Rio de Janeiro

Sao Paulo

Mendoza
Santiago

Montevideo
Buenos Aires

Oslo
Sto

Copenha

Manchester

Hamburg

Amsterc

London

Berli

Brussels

Paris

Frankf

Munich

Toulouse
Zurich

Nice
Milan

Barcelona
Rome

Madrid

Lisbon

Agadir

Dakar

Lagos

· Moscow

a
el Aviv

· Delhi

· Bahrain
· Dubai

· Bombay

· Seoul

· Tokyo

· Taipei
· Honk Kong

· Manila

· Bangkok
· Ho Chi Minh City

· Kuala Lumpur
· Singapore

airobi

· Djakarta

· Bali

re
· Port Louis
sburg

· Papeete

· Sydney
· Melbourne

· Auckland

FOREWORD

In the eternal battle between the passenger and the airlines, no arena is more important than airfares. Airfares are also the arena in which the opposing sides are most unequal.

On the one side is the full-time airline Goliath, armed with arbitrary restrictions designed to be failed by those who can afford to pay, sophisticated computer programs constantly repricing the next seat as high as the market will bear, international cartels dedicated to limiting competition and maintaining prices, misleading discount fare ads with the small print missing, commissioned phone operators chirpily guiding you towards the most expensive ticket, and so on.

On the other side is you, the hapless part-time traveler, who have a vague feeling you are being ripped off, but lack both the time and the experience to know what to do about it.

The only way you will have any hope of zapping the airline Goliath between the eyes is to fill your sling with knowledge. But finding that knowledge is extremely difficult—mainly because it is either in the hands of the people who want to charge you a high fare or in the hands of people who for one reason or another lack the ability to disseminate it.

That's why a book such as *The Worldwide Guide to Cheap Airfares* is indispensable. A book like this helps you learn how to beat the airlines at their own game—either through manipulating their practices and rules or through bypassing the airlines altogether via consolidators, courier flights and charters.

So if you are interested in raising your status from hapless part-time traveler to invincible fare warrior, start by reading this book. Now.

George Albert Brown
author, *The Airline Passenger's Guerrilla Handbook*

Dear Reader

This book is meant for the adventurous among you. Not for the arm-chair traveler, but for the bold person who wants to get out there and experience the world firsthand. Like me, you're itching to get back on the road, to get another fix of travel and thus ever-so-briefly satisfy your wanderlust.

I embarked upon this project back in 1989, out of frustration. I knew that budget travel opportunities were out there, I just didn't know how to find out about them. Today, information on cheap flights remains elusive. By and large, the companies who have access to cheap airline seats lack the ability to make themselves known. This book exists in order to teach those of you who wish to travel cheap-ly how to do it and whom to contact. It puts the right contact infor-mation at your fingertips so that you can quickly and easily reserve a cheap ticket to the destination you choose.

Some of you will remember worker-owned People Express, a small airline which pioneered low-fare, no-frills flights across the Atlantic in the early 1980s. Their plan was simple: by offering very low fares, they would attract people who never before thought they could afford to travel. People Express gained quite a following, but overex-tended itself and finally fell victim to bigger competitors. One day, a company like People Express will make long flights inexpensive again, much as Southwest and its followers have done for short hops. Until then, the secret to flying inexpensively is to use the strategies you have right here in your hands.

But don't stop traveling inexpensively the moment your plane touch-es down. Try following your cheap flight with stays at youth hostels or family-owned bed and breakfasts. Consider eating at the small, neighborhood places where the waiters still call the chef "Mom." Away from the cultural sterility of corporate-owned hotels and chain restaurants are places where the serendipity of travel flourishes, and where you'll experience chance encounters with the local people. Encourage such moments, and you will understand why I find travel so alluring. You become a welcome guest instead of a tolerated tourist.

So, the next time you travel, consider trying out the local dance, or pulling up a stool to chat at the local pub. The memory of that home-cooked meal I enjoyed with new friends in the foothills of central Morocco still makes me salivate! Keep in mind that by getting involved with the local people, you can be giving them a memorable experience as well. Maximize your chances for interactions with the people at each place you come upon, and you are bound to become addicted to this kind of travel.

Of course, you do have to get there first. But you can travel farther than you dreamed for less than you imagined, and the rest of this book shows you how.

FREE OFFER

Let me be perfectly clear here. I want you to travel. That is why I wrote this book, and why you are reading it. The more often you travel cheaply, the more people will beg you to tell them how you did it, and the more people will hear about this book. So let me make you an offer you can't refuse: use one of the strategies in the book, and take a trip. When you get back, send me a note explaining what you did, and how everything worked out. If I use your comments in the next edition of this book, I'll send you a copy of it for free!

This free book offer also extends to suggestions about whom I should list in this book. If you are the first to recommend a strategy or company that I later use in the book, I'll send you a free copy of the new edition, too. Send in the first complaint about a company that I drop, get a freebie. I need input from the thousands of readers who use these strategies. People just like you help make this book bigger, better, and more accurate with each new edition.

Send your reports, suggestions, postcards (hint hint), etc. to:

Insider Publications
2124 Kittredge Street, Third Floor
Berkeley, CA 94704 USA

e-mail: info@travelinsider.com
http://www.travelinsider.com

ABOUT THE AUTHOR

Author Michael McColl says, "Budget travel is in my blood!" A graduate of the University of California at Berkeley, he spent his junior year studying at the University of Barcelona, Spain. He claims to this day that his travels through Europe formed an integral part of his educational experience. Later, Mike returned to Europe to work as a whitewater raft guide in the Catalan Pyrenees.

Mike refined his travel writing the hard way. As one of the founding writers of Fodor's budget travel series *The Berkeley Guides,* he sweated his way through the deserts and industrial factory-towns of north-eastern Mexico. (Okay, he snuck in a review of a beach or two here and there, but only when it was absolutely necessary. . . .)

Back in Berkeley, Mike began writing *The Worldwide Guide to Cheap Airfares* in 1989. Between editions, Mike tries to justify traveling as much as possible. Using consolidator tickets, courier flights, and charters, he has traveled extensively throughout the United States, Europe, North Africa, Latin America and Asia. When not on the road researching for the next edition of *The Worldwide Guide to Cheap Airfares,* Mike makes his home in San Francisco, California.

DEMYSTIFYING BUDGET AIRFARE STRATEGIES

Beating the Airlines
at Their Own Game

Travel is an adventure. It is unpredictable, exciting, and above all, mind-opening. Travelers return home refreshed, with new stories, new perspectives, and hopefully a few new friends. Author Rick Steves calls travel "one of the last great sources of legal adventure." Yet for all its benefits, most people find themselves unable to travel as often as they would like.

The first challenge for most budget travelers is the airfare hurdle. By manipulating their carefully honed computer reservation systems, the airlines do their best to shake as much money as possible out of the consumers' pockets. But you can beat the airlines at their own game. This book will show you how.

Ever notice how you can call an airline three times and get three different prices for the same flight? Airline pricing is a complex, messy process, full of loopholes, quirks and exceptions. Most people (even most airline reservations agents) are baffled by the system. That's why most people end up paying much more than they should. However, once you begin to use the strategies outlined in this book, you can wield the weapons of the airfare market against the very airlines who created the system. Think of it as poetic justice. In trying to take our money, the airlines have made it possible for some of us to pay a lot less.

You will learn how to use discount travel "consolidators" to buy cut-rate tickets for seats the airlines fear they will be unable to sell. You will also read about charter flights, which take advantage of airline price-gouging to sell planeloads of cheap tickets to some of the world's most popular destinations. And you will learn about courier flights, where you get a steeply discounted plane ticket in exchange for carrying time-sensitive documents. When you use these strategies, you will save ten times the cost of this guide the very first time you fly.

Once you have mastered the tricks of the trade, you'll have your chance to apply them to your own globetrotting adventure. We have listed the best providers of cheap travel available in more than a dozen budget travel hub cities, worldwide. If you live in or near one of these highly trafficked, highly competitive hub cities you have a whole chapter of cheap travel options just for you. But the hub cities are listed primarily as stepping stones to cheap travel. Use them as jumping-off points, no matter what your initial departure city may be.

If you live far away from our hub cities, try to arrange your own transportation to a hub that offers cheap flights to your final destination. It is worth it to get to a hub city—most local travel agencies do not even attempt to compete with consolidator, charter, or courier prices. So instead of flying straight to Africa, consider flying through the ultimate budget travel hub city, London. You are bound to save money, and you'll get the added benefit of staying in the hub city for a day or two, if you choose. We even include a miniguide to each hub city, so that you will have enough information to enjoy a few days there while en route to somewhere else.

THE ECONOMICS OF AIRFARES

When the airlines weave their complicated web of restrictions, classes and fare codes, they have a sensible purpose in mind. They want to extract as much money as possible from the flying public.

Business travelers flying on short notice have been identified as a particularly deep-pocketed and vulnerable market, so they end up getting the worst of the airline price structure. Leisure travelers who plan their vacations months in advance (and have lots of flexibility in terms of when, where, and with which airline they fly) get much better prices. To a great extent, the fare you pay will be determined by whom the airline thinks is paying the bill. Business travelers, whose flights are paid for by their companies, will often pay whatever the airlines ask. Leisure travelers are paying out of their own pockets, so they will stay home rather than pay outrageous airfares.

No airline would dare to come right out and say that they are gouging business travelers. Instead, airlines devise all sorts of interesting restrictions, most of which (purely coincidentally, of course) make the cheapest airfares unavailable to business travelers. The theory is that few executives will stay away from home on a Saturday night just to get a cheaper fare.

You can use these restrictions to your advantage. A study reported in

George Albert Brown's *Airline Passenger's Guerrilla Handbook* found that 91 percent of U.S. air travelers paid an average of 40 percent of the full fare for their flights. That means that only 9 percent of travelers completely failed to meet the airline restrictions for lower fare tickets. So if you can purchase your tickets far enough in advance, stay over a Saturday night, stay 7 or 14 days on international flights, or fly midweek, you will pay less than full fare. But even if you can't meet the restrictions, there still are cheaper ways to fly.

On international flights, supply and demand often play second fiddle to government regulation. Under the Chicago Convention of 1944, national governments agreed to control fares for flights to or from their countries. Since many national airlines are actually owned by their governments, there is a tendency for the government-approved fares to be high. Worse yet, the governments tend to approve the fares agreed upon by the International Air Transport Association (IATA), which is a cartel made up of most of the world's airlines.

Luckily, the IATA cartel has its weaknesses, which create opportunities for cheap travel. First, IATA has no police power of its own, so it cannot enforce its official fares. Second, many countries look the other way when an airline sells seats at lower-than-official prices. The governments of the United States and Britain, for example, seem to look upon this discounting as a benefit to consumers, so they allow it to continue. In such markets, the airlines use discount travel agents to discreetly unload the seats that the airlines themselves were unable to sell. Technically, the airlines have not sold these tickets, so they can maintain their claim that they never sell seats below the official rate. Third, in countries where the government does scrupulously enforce IATA prices (as is often the case in Europe), a market for charter flights flourishes. Charter operators are not members of IATA, and therefore are not bound to IATA prices. The charter operators undercut the airline prices, and cram their planes full of budget-minded travelers.

Another good source of budget airfares is courier travel. Courier flights take advantage of a loophole in customs regulations, rather than airline restrictions. Because of a quirk in the Geneva Convention, express shipping companies must use a passenger in order to clear their packages through customs as soon as the plane lands. The shipping companies will regularly pay about half of your airfare in

3

exchange for the use of your checked baggage allowance. If you meet the requirements, courier travel is one of the best airfare bargains available today.

The following sections explain the details of discount travel agencies, charters, and courier flights. The pros and cons of each strategy are outlined, as are the most advantageous times to utilize each method. The guide then takes you across the globe, stopping at each budget travel hub city to uncover the best airfares available. Again, if your trip starts from a non-hub city, then analyze your route to determine if you might pass through one of the hubs. You will often get not only a cheaper airfare, but also a pleasant addition to your trip, if you so choose. Be creative in combining routes and strategies—it gives you a huge advantage over the airlines.

CONSOLIDATORS

Consolidators are the "factory outlet stores" of the airline industry. Just as clothing manufacturers sell excess merchandise at out-of-the-way factory outlets, the airlines sell excess seats at out-of-the-way discount travel outlets. Naturally, the airlines are very quiet about this system for discounting tickets. If everyone knew about it, the airlines would find it difficult to sell tickets at their higher, published prices. Nonetheless, savvy travelers have become increasingly aware of this savings opportunity. By using consolidators, you can fly on a major airline without sacrificing convenient scheduling or comfort. You simply will be paying hundreds of dollars less than the person next to you for the identical flight. Here's how the system works:

The laws of supply and demand say that if the airlines dropped fares to a low enough level, they would sell every single seat. (With the notable exception of Southwest Air, the airlines have claimed for years that they could not make a profit at that price level.) Southwest's success notwithstanding, most airlines continue to set fares so high that they almost never sell all the seats. On average, planes are only 66 percent full. That means that one-third of the average plane's seats are empty. This is not profitable.

Consolidators fill those empty seats for the airlines. To understand their role, think of airline seats as a perishable commodity. Each seat has some monetary value to the airline right up to departure time.

But if the seat fails to get sold before takeoff, the airline earns nothing for it. Airlines would rather earn some money for a seat than none at all. That's where the consolidators come in.

When an airline worries that some of its seats may "perish" (remain unsold at departure time), it has the option of lowering fares to attract more passengers. However, competing airlines are likely to retaliate with fare cuts of their own. This kind of airfare war is the type of thing that puts airlines into bankruptcy, so they try to avoid it. Instead, the airline often sells its excess seats at a deep discount to airfare consolidators. The consolidators mark up the tickets by about 10 percent, and sell them to retail travel agents and sometimes to the public. The airline receives some money where it otherwise would have gotten nothing, and the passenger gets to fly at a hefty discount.

Also important is how the consolidator market does *not* work. Legend has it that consolidators buy excess seats from the airlines at the last minute, and then sell them to the public for whatever they can get. This is a myth. Consolidators buy tickets one at a time, as they need them, but at a discounted price. The airlines pay attention to the large trends, and may discount based on those trends (that's why midweek flights are cheaper), but they never change prices on a single flight because it is about to take off empty.

Consolidators who sell only to other travel agents are called "wholesalers." Consolidators who sell to the public are called "bucket shops," or simply discount travel agents. There is surprisingly little difference in the price for tickets bought directly from a consolidator, and those bought from a bucket shop (who buys from a wholesaler). Frequently, a consolidator has a direct contract with one or two airlines, and uses wholesalers to buy seats on other airlines. For the sake of simplicity, we have listed only the firms that sell directly to the public, and refer to them all with the term "consolidator." In a few cases, we list agents who deal almost exclusively in consolidated tickets, but who do not have direct agreements with the airlines. We refer to these companies as "discount travel agencies."

Like clothing outlets that have to remove designer labels, consolidators often are forbidden to advertise an airline's name in conjunction with their deeply discounted fares. However, they will tell you the name of the airline by telephone when you call them. Sometimes the cheapest flights are on little-known airlines. If you feel more comfortable on a name-brand airline, ask the agent. They can often book you on another airline for only a few dollars more.

Consolidators have been called the "illegitimate children" of the airline industry—the airlines created consolidators, yet claim no knowledge of them. But these unrecognized offspring can come up with some amazing deals, if by slightly bending the airline rules here and there.

One consolidator trick is to buy tickets abroad and import them back to the traveler. Some airlines never discount in their home markets, so to get a good deal you have to look abroad. For instance, the Russian airline Aeroflot categorically discounts all of its fares to everywhere in the world—outside of Russia. The best deal for domestic travel in your country might be available only in Dubai! Some consolidators will tell you that this cannot be done, but in reality it is done every day. If you need to import a ticket, look for agents who specialize in around-the-world fares (try San Francisco and London). These agents have contracts with the airlines that give them a great deal of flexibility in constructing fares, which puts them in a good position to export tickets.

Another trick is the "local currency strategy." Where one country's currency is particularly weak against another, very good deals on international flights can be had simply by buying in the right currency. These strategies are often best left to your consolidator, although in the case of Singapore, you can walk across the causeway to Malaysia and see for yourself.

Consolidator tickets are usually as cheap or cheaper than the lowest advance purchase excursion (APEX) fare available from the airline. It makes sense to shop the airlines first, so you will know how good the consolidator prices are. The downside to consolidators is that if your flight is delayed, you may not be able to use your ticket on another airline. Nonetheless, these tickets are often your best bargain if you haven't planned ahead. If there is any chance that you may need to change or cancel your flight, consider buying trip cancellation insurance.

The safest way to buy a consolidator ticket is through your favorite travel agent. However, the agent may charge you an additional fee,

CONSOLIDATOR FARES

PROS

1 Substantial discounts on regularly scheduled airlines, especially on international routes

2 Particularly handy at the last minute, when the airlines' advance-purchase requirements would make for an unbearably high fare

3 Usually refundable, changeable tickets; often with no minimum-stay requirements

4 One-way, multi-stop, and long-stay tickets between most worldwide destinations, even on unusual and lightly traveled routes

CONS

1 Sometimes more expensive than the airlines' cheapest excursion fares during fare wars

2 Often inconvenient schedules and flights with multiple stops or circuitous routes

3 Occasional surcharge for the use of credit cards

because finding consolidator fares is time-consuming and the commission is low. To maximize savings, price shop at several consolidators.

The bucket shops listed in this guide tend to be established, larger discounters that have built up a good reputation. Smaller, local bucket shops, especially those catering to a particular ethnic group, may have similar or even better deals. If the deal seems too good to be true, call the local Better Business Bureau and check them out. And try to pay for your tickets with a credit card, so you can dispute the charge in the unlikely event that something goes wrong. If you never receive a purchased product, your credit card company will often credit the amount paid back to your account.

As mentioned, consolidators are often forbidden to advertise an airline's name when offering tickets at these low prices. This makes for a good clue when you are looking for the latest consolidator flights. Look for their tiny ads, with nothing but destinations and fares listed, in the travel section of your Sunday paper.

CHARTER FLIGHTS

Charter flights are one of the most familiar options for those who seek budget travel. These flights are the "Brand X" of the airline industry—they offer generic airline services for a less-than-brand-name price. And just as your generic corn flakes are sometimes made by one of the leading brands, your charter flight may sometimes be booked on a plane belonging to a major airline.

Charters follow seasonal increases in demand. In the summer, the crowds head to Europe, so the charter operators undercut the regular airline prices and fly thousands of people to Europe. Come wintertime, some people want to ski, while others hope to get away to someplace sunny. The charters then run to the Rocky Mountains or the Alps, and to the Caribbean or the Mediterranean. Whatever the season, the planes are full, so the fares can be lower.

Myths persist about the risks of charter flights. Every once in a while you hear of unscrupulous charter operators who suddenly disappear, leaving passengers stranded at the airport with no way to get a refund. Granted, this has happened before, but for each horror story, hundreds of thousands of passengers have enjoyed perfectly safe and reliable flights. Keep in mind, too, that scheduled airlines can also go out of business. Remember Pan Am and Eastern? As always, pay by credit card so you can dispute the charge if something goes wrong. But if you use the reputable companies listed in this book, you have very little to worry about.

The most important difference between the airlines' scheduled flights and charter flights is a legal one. When you buy a ticket with a major airline, the airline itself is legally bound to provide the services. However, when you fly a charter, your contract is not with the airline, but rather with a "tour operator." A charter tour operator rents a plane (or sections of a plane) from the airline, and then sells seats until the plane is full. If a flight is canceled, requests for refunds must be taken directly to the tour operator.

As hard as it may be to believe, the seating on charter flights can be even less comfortable than economy class on a major airline. However, the charter operators sometimes offer nonstop flights on routes where the major carriers would require a stopover or a connecting flight through the airline's hub city. In general, you should fly charter only when it offers a clear advantage over the scheduled airlines. If a charter fails to offer cheaper fares or a more direct route, then go with the more comfortable seats on a scheduled airline, and buy them at a discount from a consolidator.

Lower prices are the big selling point for charter flights. You usually save 15 to 35 percent off of typical airline fares, and you can save up to 50 percent if you book a charter flight on short notice, when there

---

CHARTER FLIGHTS

PROS

1   Entire planes full of cheap seats in high season

2   No advance-purchase requirements

3   Often the only nonstop option from a major city to a major tourist destination

CONS

1   Cramped, "cattle-car" seating, made worse by extremely full planes

2   Very long, tedious check-in lines for many charter flights

3   Irregular flight schedules, including infrequent flights and odd departure times

4   Limited to peak travel times and popular destinations

5   One-way flights often not available

are no discount tickets left on the major airlines. Charter prices offer the greatest savings during high season. Charters may be your best bet if you are headed to ski country, Hawaii, or the Caribbean this winter, or between North America and Europe this summer. Similarly, European travelers will find an abundance of charter fares available from cold northern areas to the beach resorts of Greece and southern Spain.

You can buy seats on a charter flight from most travel agents, although full-fare travel agents are unaccustomed to looking for these flights, and sometimes need to be prodded. Discount travel agents will often offer charter fares in conjunction with their steeply discounted scheduled flights. In fact, some discounters have been criticized for selling charter seats without informing the passenger that it is a charter flight. This is rare, but if the distinction is important to you, ask. Space-available or "standby" tickets are often sold on charters, since in order to be profitable, charter operators need to sell almost every seat on the flight.

As with any form of budget travel, the more flexible you are when booking a charter flight, the more money you are likely to save. A charter may not have flights every day of the week. But give them a couple of possible dates, and they are likely to save you a bundle.

THE AIR COURIER PATH TO CHEAP TRAVEL

Carry documents for an international shipping company and save about half of your airfare? It sounds too good to be true. But it happens every day, and has been going on now for about 30 years. Once you have flown as a courier, you may never pay regular over-the-counter fares again.

Courier flights have always had a cultlike popularity among the savviest of travelers. Yet courier travel is now becoming almost mainstream. *The Wall Street Journal* reports that travelers can cut the cost of international flights by 50 to 85 percent by taking advantage of courier flights.

When word first got out about air courier flights, insiders worried that their secret gravy train of cheap airfares would be derailed. There were few courier flights available, and increased passenger demand would overwhelm the supply of cheap seats. This was in the mid-eighties. Rather than dying out, courier opportunities have increased dramatically. A flock of new courier firms and brokers sprouted in the late eighties, and the larger companies are still expanding their networks as of mid-1996. Business depends more and more each year on guaranteed overnight shipping, so the need for couriers should do nothing but increase continuously for the foreseeable future.

According to *U.S. News & World Report*, about 25,000 courier flights depart American cities each year. Similar patterns exist in Europe and the Pacific Rim, so the true number of courier opportunities in a given year may approach 100,000 flights. In short, there are plenty of courier flights available for those who know how to sign up for them.

WHAT IS A COURIER?

An air courier is a person who delivers packages for companies that are in the international overnight shipping business. Typically, the courier must give up his or her checked baggage allowance for the shipping company's mailbags. In exchange, the courier gets a free or discounted air ticket.

WHY DO THE COURIER COMPANIES DO IT?

We've all heard about those international air freight services, the ones that promise to deliver your package to any place in the world, "overnight, guaranteed!" These companies (Federal Express, DHL, etc.) tend to handle an enormous volume of parcels, especially from one regional center to another. So it is usually cost-effective for them to use their own planes to carry the shipment. But when a company has only a few letters (or at most a couple of mailbags) to send, it is not cost-effective to fly a whole 747 to a distant city. Instead, the shipping service turns the packages over to an air courier company.

Courier companies are the clearinghouses of the express shipping business. They handle the small quantities of overnight freight that the big shipping companies don't want to deal with. Because overnight shipping is in great demand, courier services deliver at least a few items every day to the cities they specialize in.

Commercial airline seats are the cheapest way to move small quantities of freight quickly. An advance purchase airfare (which allows the passenger to check two pieces of luggage) is relatively inexpensive. On days when there is more than two bags' worth of freight, the firm can check the rest as excess baggage, which will still get on the plane with the passenger. Further, upon arrival in a foreign country, passenger baggage is handled faster than cargo. The edge may be only an hour or two, but that can be the difference between overnight and second-day delivery. Largely for this reason, courier companies reserve airline space every day of the week to each of their destination cities.

Of course, courier companies still could use the freight service that all major airlines provide. But there is another problem. All packages must go through customs at the destination country. Unattended packages tend to languish in a customs warehouse somewhere (sometimes for days), until the local customs officials finally get around to inspecting them. If, however, a package is accompanied through the airport as the luggage of a responsible individual traveler, it clears customs almost immediately.

This is where you come in: courier companies need individuals like you to accompany their mailbags through customs. They have to get the packages from Point A to Point B as quickly as possible. In fact, they need you so badly that they will willingly pay about half of your airfare! In exchange, they get to use part or all of your checked baggage allowance.

SO WHAT'S THE CATCH?

To get a courier flight, you must first be willing to fly (and return) when the courier company has an available seat. (Of course, the same case is true when you fly on a standard, full-fare airline ticket.) Then, you must be willing to let the courier company use your checked baggage allowance. And you will find only international courier flights, since on domestic flights there are no customs checkpoints through which shippers would need their mailbags accompanied.

What about the clothes and other belongings that you'll want to take with you? It is true that the courier company generally will use your entire checked luggage allowance to transport their mailbags. However, you get to use your entire carry-on allowance for your personal gear. As a general rule, couriers on flights to or from the United States can bring one bag (weighing less than 20 kilograms, or 44 pounds) to be placed in the overhead compartments, as well as a second bag (length + width + height = less than 45 inches) to be placed under your seat. On other flights, couriers may be restricted to one carry-on bag weighing less than 20 kilograms. This should be plenty of space for the efficient traveler's belongings. And remember, there is no rule about how much clothing you can wear onto the plane. If your bulky sweaters and coats do not fit into your carry-ons, wear them onto the plane. At your seat, peel off the excess layers and put them in the overhead bins, or into a spare nylon bag you just happen to have in your pocket.

To be a courier, you need to be adventurous and flexible. For example, you don't get your ticket until you arrive at the airport meeting point. If you are a worrier, this may not be the best option for you.

While courier travel is usually hassle-free, there are occasional foulups. Your contact person may not arrive at the meeting point precisely on time. Worse yet, on very rare occasions, couriers have been bumped to the next day, or their tickets have gotten to the airport too late. If you are an inflexible, risk-averse traveler, do not fly courier. But remember that even the major airlines occasionally cancel flights.

If you do fly courier, bring the local telephone numbers of the courier company with you on your flight, so you can call in if there is a problem. You might wish to bring the name of the local courier company written in the local language. Also, remember that the airline employees are very familiar with the whole courier procedure. If you cannot find your contact, ask the people at the airline check-in counter.

HOW DO I KNOW I'M NOT SMUGGLING CONTRABAND?

This is the first question people ask when the subject of courier travel comes up. People conjure up images of overcoat-clad strangers with aluminum attaché cases handcuffed to their sides, handing them the package that lands an innocent traveler in a Third World prison. If this sound about right, you've been watching too much late-night television.

Air courier companies are established businesses that handle only legitimate freight. They have to vouch for the contents of the mail-bags on every flight. If one package contained contraband, the entire time-sensitive shipment could be held indefinitely as evidence. The companies could not afford the loss of reputation that this would cause; a courier company caught smuggling would never get anoth-er customer. In order to guarantee to their customers the complete security of the shipment, they usually don't let you even touch the mailbags.

What's more, the bags are usually sealed, so that you could not eas-ily open them even if you were allowed to handle them. As a further precaution, many courier companies routinely x-ray all packages in order to detect contraband. When something suspicious is found, they alert customs at the departure point, and the rest of the ship-ment is allowed to proceed without delay.

Every customs agent we interviewed agreed that there is virtually no risk of being stopped for possession of contraband while working as a freelance air courier. Not a single agent had heard of a case where a courier was caught unknowingly smuggling contraband. Apparently, the smugglers prefer to use their own people for such purposes.

We spoke with United States Customs Service Public Affairs Officer Mike Fleming in order to get the official word on this issue. True to his role as a law enforcement official, he warned travelers to avoid suspicious situations. "If someone approaches you informally at the airport and asks you to bring a suitcase to his sister," he said, "red warning flags should pop up in your mind."

When you approach a courier company and ask them if you can fly as a courier, you have initiated the interaction. This is very different from the situation above. According to Fleming, the risk of carrying contraband as a freelance courier is "very minimal. I'm not aware of any instances of seizures involving individuals flying as couriers for a legitimate shipping company."

Both customs officials and airline employees are extremely familiar with the courier clearance procedure, which they perform daily. They are in a good position to give an impartial opinion on the matter of courier safety, and across the board they report that courier travel is safe. In fact, you probably have much more to fear from the airline food than you do from the cargo you are accompanying.

HOW TO TRAVEL WITH A COMPANION

Courier companies generally offer only one seat on each flight. That can make it hard to travel with a companion. However, with a little planning, it's fairly easy for two or more travelers to take advantage of these great money-saving flights. One option is to book with a courier broker. Brokers deal with several different courier companies and may have two courier seats on the same flight on the same day.

Another option is for each of you to fly the same courier route on consecutive days. The first to arrive can handle such details as getting the hotel room and reconnoitering the city, so that everything is ready when the second person arrives. This can be a minor inconvenience, but it is worth the dramatic savings on the airfare.

Of course, if your companion is being stubborn or inflexible, he or she can always pay full coach fare, and book on the same flight on which you will act as a courier. Better yet, get your companion a consolidator ticket for the same flight. It will not be as cheap as your courier fare, but you both will have saved a bundle.

ON THE DAY OF THE FLIGHT...

On your day of departure, you must be at the company's designated meeting point about two hours before the flight. Some companies simply arrange to have you meet their agent right at the airport. Others require their couriers to go to the courier company offices, from which they are escorted by a company employee to the airport.

The agent will stand in line with you at the airport, check you onto the flight, and give you your instructions and the document pouch. The pouch contains the shipping manifests, which are an official listing of the contents of the mailbags you are accompanying. In most cases, you never actually touch any mailbags—for security reasons, the company's staff checks those directly onto the plane.

You board the plane and fly just like any other passenger. (Well, you may be smiling a little more, since you know you paid much less than everyone else did.) When you arrive at your destination, you walk

15

through customs, hand the pouch to the courier representative at the airport, and you're on vacation! The company's local staff handles the mailbags, so you don't even have to wait for your baggage at the carousel. Sometimes you may not even have to meet anyone at the destination airport. Some companies now ask you to call their local office from a pay phone once you have cleared customs.

In some Third World countries, and in a few stubborn industrial nations as well, you still may be required to go to the baggage carousel, recover all of the mailbags, and roll them on a cart through customs. This is rare, but is simple enough and certainly worth the savings.

On the way home, you often have no courier duties. That means you have full use of your checked luggage space to bring home all those souvenirs. If your flight involves round-trip courier duties, you follow the same procedure as you did on the first half of the trip.

DIFFERENT COMPANIES, DIFFERENT POLICIES

There is a great deal of variability in the policies of the twenty or so courier companies listed in this guide. Some companies use only the space of one of your checked bags, while others use your entire checked baggage allotment. Similarly, some companies use your ser-vices only on the trip to your destination, while others take up your baggage allowance on your return trip as well. Some give you a huge discount off the regular airfare (up to 85 percent off), while others reduce the fare as little as possible while still filling all of their flights.

Lastly, most companies allow only short, fixed-length stays at your destination, while a few are extremely flexible about your return. The simpler logistics of making all courier assignments one week long are attractive to the courier companies; they automatically know who will be covering each return flight. Nonetheless, longer stays seem to be the wave of the future, as courier companies compete with each other for the limited pool of travelers who know about courier flights.

THE SECRET OF FLYING FREE

Courier companies usually charge you about half of the coach fare for your flight. However, sometimes a courier cancels a reservation at the last minute. This puts the courier company in a real bind, but it can be a great opportunity for you. When someone cancels more than two days before the flight, the company will try to sell the seat, often at a hefty discount. (Look for companies who offer last-minute discounts in the courier listings, below.)

In the end, someone must accompany those mailbags. The company wants to avoid sending an employee, because it would have to pay the hotel and meal costs—plus wages—while that employee is abroad.

Instead, the company will cut its losses, and send an independent courier for free! To get in on this deal, you must be willing to fly on less than 48 hours' notice. These offers happen frequently. Sometimes you have to be lucky and call them at the right time in order to take advantage of a cancellation that just occurred. Other companies keep an index card file of people who are willing to fly to

C O U R I E R   F L I G H T S

P R O S

1   Extremely cheap airfare

2   Less baggage to carry—with carry-ons only, you can skip the whole baggage carousel experience, and get on with your vacation

3   Occasional VIP treatment by airline employees

C O N S

1   Usually no checked baggage allowance

2   Tickest often nonrefundable and non-changeable

3   Limited choice of schedules and destinations

4   Often restrictions on length of stay (1–4 weeks)

5   Minimum age of 18 years on some flights

a particular destination at the last minute. These companies will actually call you and ask you if you are interested in filling their suddenly available flight. Because the person who cancelled forfeits any prepayment, you have the chance to fly cheap, and maybe even free.

If these impromptu flights interest you, call the companies who offer a last-minute phone list (see courier company listings, in the next section) and tell them that you are available. Couriers who have previously flown with that courier company will have priority, since they have proven themselves to be reliable, but first-time couriers may also be accepted. Keep a bag packed—sometimes they call you the same day!

Another option, if you are feeling especially adventurous, is to call around to see if any company has a cancellation that it needs to fill. If you just want to get away, and destination doesn't matter, you can usually find something. And you can't beat the price! Last-minute flights are most common in the low season, or on holiday weekends. From mid-May to September, the system is overloaded with students, making your chances for catching a last-minute flight much slimmer. If you want to fly courier in the summertime, try to book as early as possible.

How to Use the
Budget Travel Directory

If you already have a destination in mind, look it up in the index starting on page 231 to find out what companies will get you there. The
directory is organized by budget travel hub city, and frequently, the
hub city with the most connections to a given destination is also one
of the cheapest stepping stones to that destination. So if the direct
flights from your nearest hub city fail to meet your needs, be creative—consider paths through other convenient hubs as viable (and
often superior) alternatives to direct flights.

The hub cities are organized by region: North America, Europe, and
Asia and Australia. Within the regions, each hub city has its own
chapter that lists the companies with the cheapest airfares on departures from that city.

THE MINIGUIDES

Our **Miniguides** provide a brief introduction to each hub city. The
Market Trends section explains the conditions in the local airfare
market, such as the likelihood of finding discount travel agents there,
and particularly good deals typically available from that hub.

Residents of a particular hub can skip the rest of that city's miniguide.
It is written for travelers unfamiliar with the city who are using it as a
jumping-off point for further travel. The miniguides provide the traveler who is **Stopping Over** with enough budget travel information
to make for a short but pleasant stay in each hub. We track down the
city's **Cheap Sleeps** and **Cheap Eats** for you, and point out details
for getting **To and From the Airport**. Finally, we suggest one
Unique thing to do in each hub—one interesting (but not tourist-
infested or "typical") activity that will help give you a flavor of the city.

COMPANY LISTINGS

The company listings themselves provide most of the information you
will need. However, once you have chosen a company, make sure you
get all the details from them directly. It is your responsibility (and good
common sense) to have the latest, most complete information before
you buy your tickets or sign any agreements.

The **Address** information is provided for your convenience, but we encourage you to contact companies by telephone only. Most companies prefer that you contact them by telephone, and are very slow to respond by mail or fax, if they respond at all. Especially in the case of courier companies, communicating by telephone demonstrates that you understand how the industry works.

Telephone and Fax numbers appear in the format "(city code) number" [example: ☎ (0171) 555 1212]. If you are calling from outside the country, you should drop any zeros at the start of the city code, and dial the international access code and country code before dialing the number [example: ☎ 011 44 (171) 555 1212]. The country code is listed in the miniguide to each city. Because more and more people are finding their way onto the "information superhighway," **Internet** addresses are now provided where available. Some providers have developed intricate World Wide Web pages, while others are just now figuring out e-mail. Either way, if they have it, we list it.

A **Contact** is listed if the company is large and a particular person is responsible for booking flights.

Times to Call are important since some companies handle incoming calls only at specific times, and others may have nontraditional office hours. If an informational recording is available, we indicate that here as well.

The **Type of Provider** item tells you whether this company is a discount travel agent, a charter company, or a courier company, and whether they are a full-fledged courier company or a booking agent for such a company.

The **Areas of Specialty** listing helps you focus on companies operating from a certain hub city to the region of your choice. If a company does not specialize, we enter the term "worldwide" here. Sometimes the best fares are found through companies that specialize in a particular geographic region. Use the "areas of specialty" listing to limit your search to a few good choices. Then call them and let them know that you are serious, and will buy if the price is right. Nobody in this business has time to figure out the absolute best deal on a complicated itinerary for someone who is "just looking."

The **Destinations** chart provides you with the destinations served by each company from the hub city. In the case of charter operators and discount travel agents with too many flights to list, we provide a representative sample for your convenience.

Sample Round-Trip Fares are just that—they merely represent the kind of discounts you can expect from each of the companies listed. All sample fares are based on figures quoted by the listed companies for May 1996. These fares will change over time, so it is up to you to call and obtain current fares. Last-minute fares can be even cheaper. The sample fares don't include applicable departure taxes. If "n/a" appears under Sample Round-Trip Fare, this flight had been offered before, but was not available at press time. Call the company to check whether the flight has been resumed. Similarly, a "tba" under Sample Round-Trip Fare means that the fare is to be announced.

Full Coach Fares are supplied as a basis for evaluating the sample fares provided by listed companies. The Full Coach Fares were obtained courtesy of *The Official Airline Guides Electronic Edition Travel Service*. These fares are the cheapest published standard economy fares with minimal or no advance purchase or minimum stay requirements, as available for round-trip travel in May 1996. Where possible, we list the year-round full coach fare, rather than the constantly changing sale fares.

Which brings us to an important point: the sample fares (and discount fares in general) do change constantly. However, they do not vary much relative to full coach fares. A 50 percent savings off of full coach fares will probably remain unchanged even as full coach fares themselves rise and fall. Because our strategies save you money both when fares are high and when fares are low, a good deal today will likely still be a good deal tomorrow.

For courier companies, we also list the **Length of Stay** for each flight. As mentioned in Chapter 1, courier assignments usually last for a fixed period of time (e.g. two weeks). If there is flexibility in booking your return flight, we indicate the range of possibilities (e.g. 7 to 30 days). If we use commas and/or the word "or," then you have limited flexibility in return dates (e.g. 7, 9 or 14 days).

The area below the chart is loaded with useful tidbits of information.

For instance, **Annual Fee** refers to the charge that some courier companies impose on you for the privilege of using their services. You may want to avoid these companies unless they still offer the lowest fare even after you figure in the fee.

A **Deposit** serves as a guarantee to a courier company that you will show up for both halves of your flight. It is often paid by credit card, and refunded upon your return. Do not, under any circumstances, fail to comply with your obligatory courier duties on the return flight. It puts the courier company in the nearly impossible situation of having to find a courier on a few hours' notice. Last-minute cancellations have two effects: first, you get blacklisted by that company (and probably others) and will likely never again be accepted for a courier flight; second, some companies get fed up with freelance couriers, and stop using them entirely.

Payment Methods are outlined for you—we suggest you favor companies that allow you to pay by credit card. In the rare event that something goes wrong with your ticket, your credit card company can get you a refund. When possible, use a local company—it is usually easier to resolve any questions or problems that may arise. By all means, please notify us by mail if you ever have any problems with any of the companies listed in this guidebook.

If the listing indicates that you have no **Courier Duties on Return Trip**, you may be able to check luggage or change the dates for your return flight.

Many courier companies require that their couriers be of a certain age. If that is the case, we indicate it under **Minimum Age.**

The **In Business Since** heading tells you the date a company was founded, which can help indicate its stability in the marketplace.

It is wise to reserve your courier flight as early as possible. To this end, we include a date range called **Recommended Advance Reservations**. The first half of the date range notes how far in advance you should book so as to get the date you want. Availability is still adequate this far in advance. The second half of the date range denotes the farthest in advance that you could possibly make a reservation. No company will let you reserve a seat more than a year ahead of time, but many open their books about three months before each

22

flight. If you call on the earliest possible day, you are likely to get exactly the flight you want. As always, you can call at the last minute too, but you will be looking for cancellations, not picking the date of your choice.

If there is a special **Luggage** allowance or restriction, we let you know about it here. Remember, most courier flights allow you to bring carry-on luggage only.

If there are one-way courier flights, last-minute discounts, standby flights, or cancellation phone lists, we'll tell you in the comments section. Other interesting facts and pieces of information about the company are listed here as well.

A NOTE ABOUT CHANGE

Keep in mind that flights, destinations, and prices are constantly changing. The fares listed are meant to illustrate the savings you can expect to receive, but the actual prices will vary. Call the companies to get their current prices. Also, agencies do come and go. The agencies we have listed here are well-established, experienced operations that are consistently able to offer better deals than the airlines themselves. That much, we can promise you, will not change.

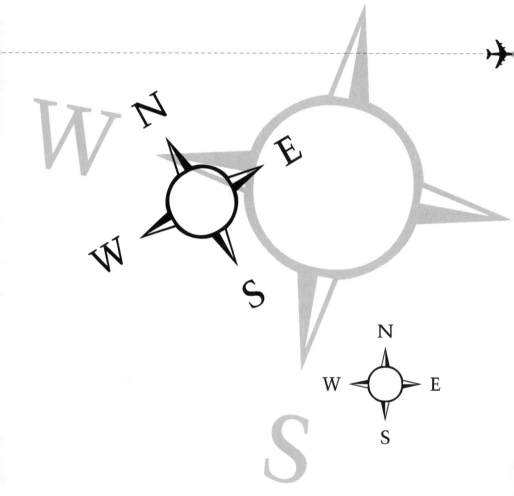

CHICAGO, U.S.A.

MARKET TRENDS

By reclaiming Midway airport, carriers like Kiwi, American Trans Air, and Midway Airlines have made domestic flights from Chicago surprisingly affordable. Courier flights are also available to London, Mexico City, and several cities in Asia. Ethnic specialty agencies offer consolidated fares to Asia and Central Europe. Most foreign tourists need an onward ticket to get into the United States.

CHAPTER 3

STOPPING OVER IN CHICAGO

The **Loop** is the strategic center of Chicago. Business, government and culture congregate here, in the area that was once served by a "loop" of trolley cars. Now it is the "El," or elevated train, which transports commuters from the many suburbs into downtown.

Gusts do swirl off Lake Michigan and through the dense forest of skyscrapers in the Windy City, but the metropolis actually owes its nickname to windbag politicians. One local describes Chicago weather as the worst of both worlds: whiteouts that can shut the whole city down in the winter, and near-body-temperature heat with 98 percent humidity in the summer.

Maybe it's due in part to the weather that the blues is such a force in Chicago. The Windy City has arguably the best live music scene in North America. The city has even named a street after venerable blues man Muddy Waters. Grab a copy of *Chicago Magazine* for details on the city's innumerable nightspots, including a list of who's playing.

For a good (but increasingly touristy) taste of those famous Chicago blues, check out the **Kingston Mines** [2548 North Halsted, ☎ (312) 477 4646, across the street from more neighborhood-oriented **B.L.U.E.S.** in Lincoln Park]. Also in the Lincoln Park/DePaul area is **The Big Nasty** [2242 North Lincoln Avenue, ☎ (312) 404 1535]. Here the 25-and-under set can run wild with their fraternity party fantasies amidst the beer, Jell-O shots, and yes, Silly String. All of these clubs are in easy walking range of the Fullerton El stop.

At night, the mobs descend on **Rush Street**, in the southern part of the Gold Coast. The singles scene is so overwhelming that the

TELEPHONE COUNTRY CODE:
(1)
CURRENCY:
Dollar
US$1 = £0.66
£1 = $1.51

Chicago police close down **Division Street** on some weekends, allowing the crowds to spill over into the streets. Take the El to the Clark-Division station, because you won't find parking in this area. **Butch McGuire's** [20 West Division Street at North Dearborn, ☎ (312) 337 9080] is the bar that started it all. Butch claims that since it opened in 1961 his bar has made possible the meeting and marriage of over 6,500 couples.

To catch a glimpse of the frenetic activity at **The Chicago Board of Trade** [141 West Jackson Boulevard], just pop into the visitor's center on the fifth floor. This is the largest commodities futures exchange in the world—watch as the wheat futures fly, and brokers frantically signal "Buy. Buy! Uh-oh! SELL! SELL! FOR THE SAKE OF GOD, SELL!" Watch the drama unfold during free tours, offered every morning on the hour.

For a great view of the Chicago skyline, climb the **John Hancock Center** [875 North Michigan Avenue] instead of the Sears Tower. You won't find tourists blocking your view, and the sunsets from Hancock's 94th floor observation deck are remarkable. Since there is a fee for the observation deck, many folks head up to the 96th floor **Images Lounge**, where they can get a drink and a view for the same price. Or you might rent a bike and explore the 26 miles of waterfront bicycle paths along Lake Michigan. **Lincoln Park** is a great place to start.

CHEAP SLEEPS

Arlington House International Hostel
616 West Arlington Place
Chicago, IL 60614 USA
☎ (800) HOSTEL 5, (312) 929 5380
Fax 312/ 665 5485

Located four blocks from the lake in upmarket **Lincoln Park**—where the young, trendy locals hang out—the hostel is walking distance from live reggae, rock and blues venues. The hostel itself has occasional parties for guests, and maintains a friendly atmosphere. There are common lounges (including one with a juke box hidden in the basement), a shared kitchen, and barbecues on Sundays. The hostel shares the building with a retirement home, an arrangement that

both sides seem to enjoy. Dorm rooms go for $13 with Rucksacker,
AAIH, IYHF or ISIC cards, or $16 without. Private rooms are $30 single, $34 double, and should be reserved two days in advance. One
word of warning—don't forget your shower sandals. This is a beautiful building in a great neighborhood, but the bathrooms are filthy.
No curfew, no lockout.

International Youth Hostel

6318 North Winthrop Avenue
Chicago, IL 60660 USA
☎ (312) 262 1011

Dorm beds go for $13 a night at this impeccably clean, friendly 125-
bed hostel. Private rooms are $40 but they fill up quickly (you can
reserve two weeks in advance by sending a money order for the first
night). There are kitchen and laundry facilities, and a communal
lounge. Located seven miles north of downtown (near the Loyola
University El station), this quiet, struggling neighborhood has its own
bars and restaurants. Lockout from 10am to 4pm, and a midnight
curfew (2am on Friday and Saturday) that they take very, very seriously (trust me. . .).

Cass Hotel

640 North Wabash Avenue
Chicago, IL 60611 USA
☎ (800) CASS 850, (312) 787 4030
Fax 312/ 787 8544

The Cass is a clean, basic older hotel. It promotes itself as being
"downtown without the downtown price." The location is indeed
both safe and central, and the premises are well maintained. All
rooms have private bath and air conditioning, and all but the very
cheapest have televisions. Rooms range from $45 for a single bed
and no TV to $65 for a large room decked out with TV and king-size
bed. Continental breakfast downstairs at the Cass Cafe will run you
an additional $2. Laundry services and a student discount are avail-
able. The nearest El station is Grand Avenue.

CHEAP EATS

Chicago pizza is thick, oozing with sauce and melted cheese, and delicious. We're talking up to two inches thick, which makes it impossible to eat without a knife and fork. The locals favor the dark, tattered atmosphere of **Gino's East Pizzeria** [160 East Superior Street at North Michigan, ☎ (312) 943 1124]. Go early or late in order to avoid the lines.

When it comes to late night eats, DePaul's **The Wiener Circle** [2622 North Clark Street, ☎ (312) 477 7444] is an institution. The fries, dogs, burgers and obnoxious counter staff are famous.

TO & FROM THE AIRPORT

From any terminal at O'Hare Airport, follow the CTA signs to the El station. For about $1.50 you can catch a 45-minute train to the Loop, where you can also transfer to local buses or other trains. The El runs 24 hours a day, and is the transportation mode of choice among airport employees.

From Midway Airport, you can also take the El to the Loop ($1.50). The last train departs the airport at 11pm, and the trip lasts 30 minutes.

UNIQUELY CHICAGO

To see Chicagoans (at least the North Siders) at their uninhibited best, take in a **Chicago Cubs** baseball game. The ivy-covered walls of Wrigley Field ring one of America's classic ballparks. Bleacher seats are both the cheapest and the most social, but they usually sell out far in advance. Not to worry. Our sources tell us you can always buy tickets from scalpers for as little as face value ($9) depending on the weather and the opponent. Buy a hot dog or a bag of peanuts in order to get the full effect of the experience. Those not horribly familiar with baseball may enjoy the activity in the stands as much as that on the field. Foreign travelers may find asking questions about the game to be an effective way to meet the locals, especially when the Cubs are winning. Take the El to **Wrigley Field** (Addison Street Station), and consider a stop at one of the many nearby bars for pregame "warm-ups."

Council Travel

1153 North Dearborn Street, Second Floor

Chicago, IL 60610 USA

☎ (800) 2COUNCIL, (312) 951 0585

Fax 312/ 951 7473

Internet: http://www.ciee.org/cts/ctshome.htm

Times to Call: 9am to 5pm

Type of Provider: Discount travel agency

Areas of Specialty: Worldwide

DESTINATIONS	SAMPLE ROUND-TRIP FARE	FULL COACH FARE
Amsterdam	$475	$1,418
Bangkok	$915	n/a
Frankfurt	$649	$1,408
Hong Kong	$885	$1,816
London	$649	$1,116
Singapore	$1,006	$3,112
Sydney	$1,265	$2,419
Tokyo	$839	$1,660

Payment Methods: Cash, money order, personal check, Visa, MasterCard

In Business Since: 1947

The Council on International Educational Exchange (CIEE) is a non-profit organization dedicated to the pursuit of work, study and travel abroad. Council's roots are in student travel, which still makes up the bulk of its business. However, there has been a trend in recent years towards offering more programs for the general public.

Founded in 1947, CIEE initially got students to Europe by sea, using recycled World War II troop ships provided by the U.S. government. From these humble beginnings, it has grown into the largest operator of charter flights from the U.S. to Europe. CIEE has incorporated two travel companies, Council Travel and Council Charter. Council Travel will book you on the cheapest flight they can find for you, whether it's a Council Charter flight (America's oldest charter company), another company's charter flight, or a discounted ticket on a scheduled airline. Some interesting Council Charters run from New York to Rome or Amsterdam.

CIEE comprises 210 members worldwide, mostly universities. In 1967 CIEE began offering programs for studying or working abroad. If you are interested in such programs, contact Council Travel. They can guide you through the web of governmental red tape, and make your international experience easier. Council Travel also sells travel gear, rail passes and student IDs.

Cut Rate Travel

1220 Montgomery Drive

Deerfield, IL 60015 USA

☎ (800) 388 0575, (847) 405 0575

Fax 847/ 405 0587

Times to Call: 8am to 7pm, seven days a week

Type of Provider: Consolidator

Areas of Specialty: Worldwide except the USA and Canada

DESTINATIONS	SAMPLE ROUND-TRIP FARE	FULL COACH FARE
Amsterdam	$479	$1,418
Buenos Aires	$979	$1,536
Budapest	$679	n/a
Frankfurt	$489	$1,408
London	$479	$1,116
Moscow	$679	$1,628
Paris	$439	$1,408
Rio de Janeiro	$989	n/a
Rome	$496	$1,458
San Jose	$479	n/a
Sydney	$1,099	$2,419
Tel Aviv	$850	$1,680

Payment Methods: Cash, personal check, Visa, MasterCard, American Express

In Business Since: 1982

99.9 percent of all agencies do domestic flights—Cut Rate does not, except for connections on international flights. They are true international specialists.

Cut Rate stays open evenings and weekends in order to make things more convenient for travelers. They also have special deals for students, those traveling on short notice, and people who need a one-way flight.

Halbart Express

1475 Elmhurst
Grove Village, IL 60009 USA
☎ (847) 806 1250
Contact: Julie or Scott

Times to Call: 1pm to 4pm only, CST
Type of Provider: Courier company
Areas of Specialty: Worldwide

DESTINATIONS	SAMPLE ROUND-TRIP FARE	FULL COACH FARE	LENGTH OF STAY
London	$300	$1,116	7 or 8 days
Mexico City	flights discontinued until further notice		

Payment Methods: Cash, money order, personal check, Visa, MasterCard, American Express
Minimum Age: 18 years
In Business Since: 1980
Recommended Advance Reservations: 6 to 8 weeks

Courier receives full frequent-flyer miles on most flights. A departure tax of $28.50 is not included in the above rates.

International Bonded Couriers (IBC)

114 Touhy Court
Des Plaines, IL 60018 USA
☎ (800) 771 2926, (847) 699 3324

Times to Call: 9am to 5:30pm
Type of Provider: Courier company
Areas of Specialty: Asia

DESTINATIONS	SAMPLE ROUND-TRIP FARE	FULL COACH FARE	LENGTH OF STAY
Bangkok	tba		
Tokyo	tba		

Payment Methods: Cash, money order, personal check

Minimum Age: 18 years

In Business Since: 1988

Recommended Advance Reservations: 6 to 8 weeks

Japan Budget Travel

104 South Michigan Avenue, Suite 702

Chicago, IL 60603 USA

☎ (800) 843 0273, (312) 236 9797

Fax 312/ 236 8536

Times to Call: 9am to 5pm

Type of Provider: Consolidator

Areas of Specialty: Asia

DESTINATIONS	SAMPLE ROUND-TRIP FARE	FULL COACH FARE
Bangkok	$1,191	n/a
Hong Kong	$1,011	$1,816
Seoul	$1,080	$1,663
Tokyo	$820	$1,660

Payment Methods: Cash, personal check, Visa, MasterCard, American Express

In Business Since: 1987

Jupiter Air (Micom America)

224 Howard Avenue

Des Plaines, IL 60018 USA

☎ (847) 298 3850

Fax 847/ 298 3854

Contact: Elba

Times to Call: 9am to 5:30pm

Type of Provider: Courier company

Areas of Specialty: Asia

DESTINATIONS	SAMPLE ROUND-TRIP FARE	FULL COACH FARE	LENGTH OF STAY
Hong Kong	$550	$1,816	7 to 30 days
London	$350	$1,116	7 to 14 days

Deposit: $100

Payment Methods: Cash, money order, personal check

Minimum Age: 18 years

In Business Since: 1988

Recommended Advance Reservations: 6 to 8 weeks

Requires a $35 registration fee.

Mena Travel

2479 North Clark Street

Chicago, IL 60614 USA

☎ (800) 536 6362, (312) 472 5361

Fax 312/ 472 2829

Times to Call: 9am to 6:30pm

Type of Provider: Consolidator

Areas of Specialty: Latin America

DESTINATIONS	SAMPLE ROUND-TRIP FARE	FULL COACH FARE
Bogota	$591	n/a
Buenos Aires	$952	$1,536
San Salvador	$486	n/a
Guatemala City	$408	$727
Lima	$724	n/a
Mexico City	$295	$569
Rio de Janeiro	$1,030	n/a

MasterCard, American Express

In Business Since: 1965

Mena sells both to travel agents and to the public. They also offer land packages to most of Latin America.

Omega World Travel

10 South Riverside Plaza #124

Chicago, IL 60606 USA

☎ (800) 856 9224, (312) 715 0717

Fax 312/ 715 0722

Times to Call: 8am to 5pm

Type of Provider: Discount travel agent

Areas of Specialty: Europe, Middle East, domestic USA

Payment Methods: For TWA deal, accepts credit cards only.

In Business Since: 1970

By knowing to ask for the "TWA Global Discount fares," you will automatically get 20 percent off all domestic TWA fares, and 25 percent off all international fares. You get the same seat on the same flight—you just pay less. Call TWA first at ☎ (800) 221 2000 to get the flight number and lowest published fare for the flight you want, then call Omega World Travel to book the ticket. Senior and student fares are excluded from this offer. How do they do it? Under its restructuring plan, TWA owes investor Carl Icahn roughly $600 million. Carl has the right to buy TWA tickets at 40 percent or more off of published fares. He marks them up a bit and resells them, with the profit going to reduce TWA's debt. Omega buys from Carl's agent, and passes the 20 to 25 percent discount on to you. This deal will continue until the debt is paid in full, which will probably be in 1998 or later.

We list additional Omega offices in the Los Angeles, New York, and San Francisco chapters. Not near one of these cities? No problem. Omega has 280 offices nationwide. Call (800) 955 2582 to find the office nearest you.

Skylink Travel

30 North Michigan Avenue, Suite 1015

Chicago, IL 60602 USA

☎ (800) 433 3161 (Chicago area only), (312) 263 7664

Fax 312/ 263 0587

Times to Call: 9am to 6pm

Type of Provider: Consolidator

Areas of Specialty: Europe, Africa, Middle East, India

DESTINATIONS	SAMPLE ROUND-TRIP FARE	FULL COACH FARE
Amsterdam	$630	$1,418
Bombay	$1,200	$1,736
Lagos	$1,299	n/a
London	$630	$1,116

Paris	$640	$1,408	
Tel Aviv	$899	$1,680	

Payment Methods: Cash, money order, certified check, personal check. Will accept credit cards in person only.

In Business Since: 1982

Additional offices in Los Angeles, New York, and Washington, DC. The majority of their business is sales to travel agents. Have your dates, departure city and destination ready before you call.

STA Travel

429 South Dearborn Street

Chicago, IL 90024 USA

☎ (800) 777 0112, (312) 786 9050

Fax 312/ 786 9817

Internet: http://www.sta-travel.com/

Times to Call: 10am to 6pm

Type of Provider: Discount travel agency

Areas of Specialty: Worldwide

DESTINATIONS	SAMPLE ROUND-TRIP FARE	FULL COACH FARE
Amsterdam	$530	$1,418
Bangkok	$925	n/a
Frankfurt	$555	$1,408
Hong Kong	$870	$1,816
London	$496	$1,116
Singapore	$945	$3,122
Sydney	$1,016	$2,419
Tokyo	$869	$1,660

Payment Methods: Cash, money order, certified check, personal check, Visa, MasterCard, American Express

In Business Since: 1975

STA is the world's largest travel organization for students and young, independent travelers. They have 120 locations worldwide. Some of their best fares require student ID, or carry a maximum age.

Their tickets are highly flexible, usually good for one year, and require no advance purchase. Date changes can be made at any office world-wide for $25; refunds cost only $75. Such flexible tickets are a wise choice for travelers going on long trips without fully concrete itineraries. STA tickets are priced based on one-way tickets, which makes it easy to book open-jaw flights.

UniTravel Corp.
1177 North Warson Road
St. Louis, MO 63132 USA
☎ (800) 325 2222
Fax 314/ 569 2503
Internet: http://unitravel.com/ (This site is for travel agents only.)

Times to Call: 8am to 8pm weekdays, 8am to 4pm Saturday
Type of Provider: Nationwide consolidator
Areas of Specialty: Western Europe, South Africa and domestic USA

DESTINATIONS	SAMPLE ROUND-TRIP FARE	FULL COACH FARE
Atlanta to Amsterdam	$636	$1,388
Miami to Rio de Janeiro	$914	$1,450
Chicago to Johannesburg	$1,497	n/a
New York to Paris	$495	$758
San Francisco to Munich	$658	$1,558

Payment Methods: Cash, money order, certified check, Visa, MasterCard, American Express
In Business Since: 1968

OK, so these guys aren't even in Illinois. Often their fares are low enough to make it worthwhile to do business with them anyway. And while they are listed in the Chicago chapter, they sell tickets for departures from anywhere in the United States. In fact, they also sell discounted tickets with origination points in Europe and Latin America.

UniTravel is one of the most highly automated providers of discount airfares in the world. They sell primarily to retail travel agents, but they do accept calls from the public. Don't expect a lot of coaching from them—have your dates, destination and departure city ready when you call.

UniTravel consolidates for major airlines like British Airways, Air France, and Delta Airlines. They now offer good fares to South America and South Africa in addition to their European and American destinations. On their best domestic deals, there is a two-day advance purchase clause, but no Saturday night stay is required.

LOS ANGELES, USA

CHAPTER 4

MARKET TRENDS

Los Angeles is home to a robust market for consolidator, charter and courier flights. Consolidator offerings are good for Latin America and Europe, while charters are available to Europe and the Caribbean. Courier deals focus on Australia and Asia, although occasionally London flights are available. Most foreign tourists need an onward ticket to get into the United States. Pick up the Sunday "Travel" section of the *Los Angeles Times* to find ads for discount airfares.

STOPPING OVER IN LOS ANGELES

"The City of Angels," while technically the proper translation, is really a misnomer for Los Angeles. The City of Autos might be more accurate. In order to survive for any length of time here, you should consider obtaining a vehicle. The sprawling metropolitan area requires two hours to drive across, and no two attractions are within walking distance of each other.

Culturally, Los Angeles is the land of the "beautiful people." Because of the preponderance of aspiring actors, Los Angeles has some of the best-looking restaurant staffs in the world. Courtesy of the booming plastic-surgery industry, you will see plenty of healthy, wrinkle-free senior citizens cruising about in their convertible BMW's. Even the city's espresso-guzzling slackers are apt to be tan and fit in this image-before-substance enclave.

Note: 310 area codes east of the Los Angeles River will change to 562 in early 1997.

TELEPHONE COUNTRY CODE:

(1)

CURRENCY:
Dollar
US$1 = £0.66
£1 = $1.51

CHEAP SLEEPS

Santa Monica International Youth Hostel
1436 Second Street
Santa Monica, CA 90401 USA
☎ (310) 393 9913
Fax 310/ 393 1769

One of the best hostels in Los Angeles runs only $18 a night. Youth Hostel Association membership is required June through September. It's a beautiful wood-and-brick building one block from the Third

Street promenade, a fun place to hang out. 238 beds, reserve in summer. There's a good bulletin board for ride shares and whatnot. The pleasant patio area is a good place to meet other travelers.

Hostel California

2221 Lincoln Boulevard
Venice, CA 90291 USA
☎ (310) 305 0250

A private hostel that allows drinking, socializing, smoking, and mural painting. $15 a night, 74 beds, prefers international visitors, and has a ride board if you're looking to head out of Los Angeles.

Banana Bungalow

2775 Cahuenga Boulevard
Hollywood, CA 90068 USA
☎ (800) 446 7835, (213) 851 1129
Fax 213/ 851 1569

You'll find amenities galore at this hostel—swimming pool, weight room, basketball court, cheap restaurant, free parking, and so on. Private rooms with two double beds are $45 a night for two people, $55 a night for three, or $65 for four people. Dorm rooms, with six beds each, go for $15 a night. Tax, linens and a light breakfast are included, and all rooms include bath. Hollywood Boulevard and Universal Studios are only a 15-minute walk away. Reservations are accepted for private rooms only. Get there early to get a dorm room in July and August.

CHEAP EATS

A tip from the Santa Monica International Hostel led me around the block to **The Gallerie Gourmet**, a budget diner's dream. Sixteen small stands line the halls of this food court, located next to the Cineplex Odeon [1439 Third Street Promenade, Santa Monica]. An astounding variety of cheap ethnic foods is available, from Japanese curry through Mexican and Thai cuisine, pasta, pizza, French fries and more, all for under $5 a person. There are outdoor tables for sharing.

For good, cheap-ish Caribbean food, try **Versailles** [10319 Venice Blvd. at Motor Avenue in Culver City, ☎ (310) 558 3168]. Open daily

11am to 10pm. A cool, young crowd favors the simple Cuban fare here. Not fancy, but popular.

TO & FROM THE AIRPORT

Didn't we tell you to get a car? We mean it. You simply cannot experience Los Angeles properly without one. For bonus points, consider splurging on a convertible.

From LAX, vehicularly impaired folks staying at the Airport Interclub Hostel or the Banana Bungalow can get a free ride from the airport by calling the hostel. Otherwise, to get to downtown, Hollywood or Santa Monica, catch the free shuttle bus "C" from the LAX Shuttle sign. Shuttle C runs every 10 minutes, 24 hours a day, and the ride to the RTD City Bus Center is 10 minutes. From the Bus Center, catch bus No. 439 to downtown. To Santa Monica, catch Santa Monica Transit Bus No. 3. For RTD Information, call ☎ (213) 626 4455.

A note about customs: travelers arriving at LAX with nothing to declare can save at least 90 minutes by using the "Express Line."

UNIQUELY LOS ANGELES

Stroll down Ocean Front Walk and experience the impromptu carnival that is Venice. Drop by **Muscle Beach** to see quintessential L.A. —tanned, narcissistic bodybuilders pumping large quantities of iron in an open-air, beachfront gymnasium. You'll find cheap-and-greasy food stands, if you dare, as well as an ever-changing lineup of street performers, rollerblading models (who share the Strand with a funky rollerblading rock guitarist), dancers, jugglers, and mimes. And, of course, there is the beach itself.

Bridges Worldwide

Building #197, JFK International Airport

Jamaica, NY 11430 USA

☎ (718) 244 7244

Fax 718/ 244 7240

Contact: Ruanda or Andrea

Times to Call: 9am to 5pm EST

Type of Provider: Courier company

Areas of Specialty: London

DESTINATIONS	SAMPLE ROUND-TRIP FARE	FULL COACH FARE	LENGTH OF STAY
London	$440	$1,158	up to 6 weeks

Deposit: None

Payment Methods: Cash, personal check, Visa, MasterCard

Minimum Age: 21

In Business Since: 1992

Recommended Advance Reservations: 1 to 6 months

Luggage: Carry-on and 23kg of checked luggage

A cancellation phone list is available. Bridges is handling LA bookings for Virgin Express, and is expected to add several Pacific Rim routes in the near future.

Cheap Tickets, Inc.

8320 Lincoln Boulevard, Room 101

Los Angeles, CA 90045 USA

☎ (800) 377 1000, (310) 645 5054

Fax 310/ 645 8555

Times to Call: 6am to 8pm weekdays, 9am to 3pm Saturdays

Type of Provider: Consolidator

Areas of Specialty: Hawaii, domestic USA, and international

DESTINATIONS	SAMPLE ROUND-TRIP FARE	FULL COACH FARE
Bangkok	$869	$2,270
Honolulu	$249	$620
London	$639	$1,158
Maui	$309	$638
Paris	$779	$1,558

From			
From	Sydney	$799	$1,408
Los Angeles	Tokyo	$589	$930

Payment Methods: Cash, money order, certified check, personal check, Visa, MasterCard, American Express
In Business Since: 1986

Tickets are nonrefundable and non-changeable unless specifically noted by Cheap Tickets. Additional offices in Hawaii, New York and San Francisco.

Council Travel

10904 Lindbrook Drive
Los Angeles, CA 90024 USA
☎ (800) 2COUNCIL, (310) 208 3551
Fax 310/ 208 4407
Internet: http://www.ciee.org/cts/ctshome.htm

Times to Call: 9am to 5pm
Type of Provider: Discount travel agent
Areas of Specialty: Worldwide student, youth, and budget travel

DESTINATIONS	SAMPLE ROUND-TRIP FARE	FULL COACH FARE
Amsterdam	$589	$1,558
Bangkok	$779	$2,270
Frankfurt	$595	$1,558
London	$693	$1,158
Singapore	$823	$1,080
Sydney	$882	$1,408
Tokyo	$559	$930

In Business Since: 1947
Payment Methods: Cash, money order, personal check, Visa, MasterCard

(See the Council Travel listing on page 29 in the Chicago chapter for company background.)

East West Express

PO Box 30849
JFK Airport Station
Jamaica, NY 11430 USA
☎ (718) 656 6246
Contact: Tracy

Times to Call: 9am to 5pm
Type of Provider: Courier company
Areas of Specialty: Worldwide

DESTINATIONS	SAMPLE ROUND-TRIP FARE	FULL COACH FARE	LENGTH OF STAY
Bangkok	$650	$2,270	2 weeks
Hong Kong	$650	$819	2 weeks
Johannesburg	$1,050	n/a	up to 45 days
Manila	$650	$1,420	2 weeks
Singapore	$650	$1,080	2 weeks
Sydney	$850	$1,408	7 to 90 days

Payment Methods: Cash, money order, certified check,
personal check
Courier Duties on Return Trip: Yes
Minimum Age: 18 years
In Business Since: 1989
Recommended Advance Reservations: 2 months
Luggage: Carry-on only for outbound flight. Two checked bags on
return flight.

Call to check on last-minute discounts. Couriers do not earn frequent-flyer miles, but can make date changes without penalty.

Film International

8900 Bellanca Avenue, Suite C
Los Angeles, CA 90045 USA
☎ (310) 568 8403
Fax 310/ 568 8275
Contact: Milton

Times to Call: 9am to 5pm
Type of Provider: Courier company
Areas of Specialty: Mexico City

From	DESTINATIONS	SAMPLE ROUND-TRIP FARE	FULL COACH FARE	LENGTH OF STAY
Los Angeles	Mexico City	$250	$475	up to 30 days

Deposit: $500!

Payment Methods: Cash, money order, personal check, Visa, MasterCard

Courier Duties on Return Trip: Yes

Minimum Age: 21 years

In Business Since: 1988

Recommended Advance Reservations: 4 to 6 weeks

Luggage: One piece of carry-on only

No flights on Fridays or Sundays.

Halbart Express

1016 West Hillcrest Boulevard
Inglewood, CA 90301 USA
☎ (310) 417 3048
Fax 310/ 417 9792

Times to Call: 10am to 4pm

Type of Provider: Courier company

Areas of Specialty: Worldwide

DESTINATIONS	SAMPLE ROUND-TRIP FARE	FULL COACH FARE	LENGTH OF STAY
London	$400	$1,158	7 days
Sydney	$550	$1,408	14 days

Deposit: $500!

Payment Methods: Cash, money order, personal check

Courier Duties on Return Trip: Yes

Minimum Age: 18 years

In Business Since: 1980

Recommended Advance Reservations: 4 to 6 weeks

Luggage: One piece of carry-on only

IBC Pacific (International Bonded Courier)

From

Los Angeles

1595 El Segundo Boulevard

El Segundo, CA 90245 USA

☎ (310) 665 1760

Fax 310/ 665 0247

Contact: Yolanda

Times to Call: 9am to 4pm, Tuesday through Friday
(Informational recording available after hours.)

Type of Provider: Courier company

Areas of Specialty: Pacific Rim

DESTINATIONS	SAMPLE ROUND-TRIP FARE	FULL COACH FARE	LENGTH OF STAY
Bangkok	$495	$2,270	10 days
Hong Kong	$495	$819	9 to 13 days
Manila	$495	$1,420	14 days
Singapore	$525	$1,080	10 to 12 days
Taipei	$400	$865	10 to 12 days
Tokyo	$400	$930	7 or 11 days

Deposit: $500!

Payment Methods: Cash, money order, personal check, Visa,
MasterCard

Courier Duties on Return Trip: Yes

Minimum Age: 21 years

In Business Since: 1988

Recommended Advance Reservations: 4 to 6 weeks

Luggage: One piece of carry-on only

Cancellation phone list available. Additional offices are located in
Chicago, Miami and New York. Courier receives frequent-flyer
mileage on Northwest Airlines.

Jupiter Air

460 S. Hindry Avenue Unit D

Inglewood, CA 90301 USA

☎ (310) 670 1197 or 670 1198

Fax 310/ 649 2771

Contact: Grace or Melissa

Times to Call: 10am to 3pm

Type of Provider: Courier company

Areas of Specialty: Asia

DESTINATIONS	SAMPLE ROUND-TRIP FARE	FULL COACH FARE	LENGTH OF STAY
Bangkok	$370	$2,270	up to 30 days
Hong Kong	$400	$819	up to 30 days
Seoul	$350	$1,045	up to 30 days
Singapore	$400	$1,080	up to 30 days

Annual Fee: $35 for a three-year membership

Deposit: $100

Payment Methods: Cash, money order, certified check

Courier Duties on Return Trip: Yes

Minimum Age: 18 years

In Business Since: 1988

Recommended Advance Reservations: ASAP to 3 months

Last-minute flights can be had for 50 percent off. The cancellation phone list produces rare but substantial discounts. Jupiter strongly favors repeat business. Additional offices in many of the hub cities in this book.

Hong Kong is Jupiter Air's hub city. Thus it is sometimes possible to reserve a courier flight from Hong Kong to other Asian cities, such as Bangkok or Tokyo. Keep in mind that you must be back in Hong Kong in time for your return flight.

Lima Service

15685 Hawthorne

Lawndale, CA 98216 USA

☎ (310) 219 3250

Fax 310/ 219 3426

Contact: Leila Fuentes

Times to Call: 9am to 5pm

Type of Provider: Courier company

Areas of Specialty: Lima

DESTINATIONS	SAMPLE ROUND-TRIP FARE	FULL COACH FARE	LENGTH OF STAY
Lima	$350	$899	4 to 30 days

Deposit: None

Payment Methods: Cash, money order, certified check

Minimum Age: 21

In Business Since: 1992

Recommended Advance Reservations: 4 to 6 weeks

Luggage: Carry-on only

Couriers carry no documents, but they give up their checked baggage space, which is used to ship apparel. The office staff speaks very little English, so it is useful to speak Spanish.

Midnite Express

930 West Hyde Park Boulevard

Inglewood, CA 90302 USA

☎ (310) 330 7096

Fax 310/ 671 0107

Contact: Ms. Linda Ruth

Times to Call: 9am to 10am only

Type of Provider: Courier company

Areas of Specialty: London

DESTINATIONS	SAMPLE ROUND-TRIP FARE	FULL COACH FARE	LENGTH OF STAY
London	$350	$1,158	2 wks to 6 mos

Deposit: $500!

Payment Methods: Cash, money order, certified check, personal check, Visa, MasterCard

Minimum Age: 21

In Business Since: 1988

Recommended Advance Reservations: 1 to 6 months

Luggage: Carry-on only on outbound leg, no restrictions on return

A cancellation phone list is available. Midnite Express sends only one courier per week, on Saturday. To get that coveted seat, you should call at 9am on the first day of the month, two months before you wish to fly (e.g., call May 1st to reserve July 15th). To be eligible, you must live in Southern California; that is, within the triangle created by Santa Barbara, Palm Springs, and San Diego.

New Frontiers

5757 West Century Boulevard

Los Angeles, CA 90045 USA

☎ (800) 677 0720, (310) 641 0749

Fax 310/ 338 0708

Internet: http://www.sv.vtcom.fr/nf/ (note: French language site)

Times to Call: 9am to 5:30pm

Type of Provider: Consolidator and charter operator

Areas of Specialty: Worldwide

DESTINATIONS	SAMPLE ROUND-TRIP FARE	FULL COACH FARE
Paris	$448	$1,558
Papeete	$598	$998

Payment Methods: Cash, money order, certified check, personal check, Visa, MasterCard, American Express

In Business Since: 1967

Discount tickets on Tower Air, American Trans Air, Continental, KLM, American Airlines, and CORSAIR. Started in 1967 by a French law student who was putting together a trip to Morocco for some friends, the entire trip cost a quarter of the price of a round-trip air ticket from Paris to Casablanca. Later, he organized a second trip for 300 people, and Nouvelles Frontières (as the company is known in Europe) was born. They now have 132 offices worldwide, and some of the cheapest flights to or from the French-speaking world. Pioneer discounter New Frontiers fought the airline cartel in a landmark 1985 European Court of Justice case, which set the precedent making the sale of cheap tickets in Europe possible.

Now Voyager

74 Varick Street, Suite 307

New York, NY 10013 USA

☎ (212) 431 1616

Fax 212/ 334 5243 or 219 1753

Times to Call: 10am to 5:30pm weekdays, 12pm to 4:30pm Saturday (Informational recording available from 6pm to 10am EST.)

Type of Provider: Courier broker, charter operator and standby broker

DESTINATIONS	SAMPLE ROUND-TRIP FARE	FULL COACH FARE	LENGTH OF STAY
Auckland	tba	$1,408	up to 90 days
Sydney	tba	$1,408	up to 90 days

Annual Fee: $50

Deposit: $100

Payment Methods: Cash, money order, certified check, personal check, Visa, MasterCard, American Express

Courier Duties on Return Trip: Yes

Minimum Age: 18 years

In Business Since: 1984

Recommended Advance Reservations: 1 to 3 months

Call to check on last-minute discounts. Ask about the last-minute phone list, called the Jet-Setters Roster. They claim that 95 percent of standby customers get onto their first flight.

Omega World Travel

2049 Century Park East

Los Angeles, CA 90067 USA

☎ (800) 969 1020, (310) 557 2080

Fax 310/ 557 2870

Times to Call: 8am to 5:30pm

Type of Provider: Discount travel agent

Areas of Specialty: Europe, Middle East, domestic USA

Payment Methods: For TWA deal, accepts credit cards only.

In Business Since: 1970

By knowing to ask for the "TWA Global Discount fares," you will automatically get 20 percent off all domestic TWA fares, and 25 percent off all international fares. You get the same seat on the same flight—you just pay less. Call TWA first at ☎ (800) 221 2000 to get the flight number and lowest published fare for the flight you want, then call Omega World Travel to book the ticket. Senior and student fares are excluded from this offer. How do they do it? Under its restructuring plan, TWA owes investor Carl Icahn roughly $600 million. Carl has the right to buy TWA tickets at 40 percent or more off of published fares. He marks them up a bit and resells them, with the profit going to reduce TWA's debt. Omega buys from Carl's agent, and passes the 20 to 25 percent discount on to you. This deal will continue until the debt is paid in full, which will probably be in 1998 or later.

We list additional Omega offices in the Chicago, New York, and San Francisco chapters. Not near one of these cities? No problem. Omega has 280 offices nationwide. Call (800) 955 2582 to find the office nearest you.

STA Travel

920 Westwood Boulevard
Westwood, CA 90024 USA
☎ (800) 777 0112, (310) 824 1574
Fax 310/ 824 2928
Internet: http://www.sta-travel.com/

Times to Call: 10am to 6pm
Type of Provider: Discount travel agency
Areas of Specialty: Worldwide

DESTINATIONS	SAMPLE ROUND-TRIP FARE	FULL COACH FARE
Amsterdam	$630	$1,558
Bangkok	$825	$2,270
Frankfurt	$665	$1,558
Hong Kong	$670	$819
London	$566	$1,158
Singapore	$845	$1,080
Sydney	$916	$1,408
Tokyo	$669	$930

Payment Methods: Cash, money order, certified check, personal check, Visa, MasterCard, American Express
In Business Since: 1975

STA is the world's largest travel organization for students and young, independent travelers. They have 120 locations worldwide. Some of their best fares require student ID, or carry a maximum age.

Their tickets are highly flexible, usually good for one year and requiring no advance purchase. Date changes can be made at any office worldwide for $25; refunds cost only $75. Such flexible tickets are a wise choice for travelers going on long trips without fully concrete itineraries. STA tickets are priced based on one-way tickets, which makes it easy to book open-jaw flights.

SunTrips

The SunTrips Building
2350 Paragon Drive
San Jose, CA 95131 USA
☎ (800) 786 8747, (408) 432 1101
Internet: http://www.suntrip.com/

Times to Call: 7:30am to 6:30pm weekdays, Saturday 9am to 4pm, 10am to 2pm Sunday
Type of Provider: Charter operator
Areas of Specialty: Europe, Mexico and domestic USA

DESTINATIONS	SAMPLE ROUND-TRIP FARE	FULL COACH FARE
Boston	$218	$673
Cancun	$229	$690
Kauai	$289	$1,100
Honolulu	$219	$620
Maui	$239	$638
Puerto Vallarta	$149	$544

Payment Methods: Cash, money order, certified check, personal check, Visa, MasterCard, American Express
In Business Since: 1976

SunTrips' coast-to-coast and London flights operate in spring and summer only, except for the Los Angeles to Boston run.

Hawaii and coast-to-coast flights are scheduled service. Mexico and London are charter flights. London flights use Stansted Airport, which has a direct rail link to the London Underground's Liverpool Station. Most aircraft are provided and operated by Leisure Air, a major charter company. Book Los Angeles flights with your local travel agent, or call their central office in San Jose.

MIAMI

CHAPTER 5

MARKET TRENDS

Miami is the connecting point between Latin American and North American business. This makes for a fabulous variety of courier flights from Miami south. How about flying from Miami to Caracas, Venezuela round trip for $100? Miami also benefits from an increasingly competitive domestic air travel market all along the East coast, which makes $99 flights to New York possible. Peak season in Miami itself runs from Christmas through the college spring breaks in late March. Prices and hostel occupancy are at their height at this time. Most foreign tourists need an onward ticket to get into the United States.

STOPPING OVER IN MIAMI

Miami's **South Beach** (those in the know call it "SoBe") is quickly gaining a reputation as the American Riviera. Photogenic Art Deco buildings and palm-lined beaches provide quite a backdrop for galleries, restaurants, and visitors from all over the world. Most of the district is listed in the National Register of Historic Places.

The South Beach area was the place to be in the twenties and thirties, when wealthy Cubans and sun-hungry northerners made their annual migrations to see and be seen. The area lost its popularity in subsequent decades, and the famous Art Deco buildings began to deteriorate. The plus side to this fall from grace was the birth of a budget lodgings sector with unsurpassed scenery. The palm trees, the beaches and the pastel-stuccoed hotels were still there, and the backpacker set could afford to enjoy them. Sadly, this may change by the end of the decade.

TELEPHONE
COUNTRY CODE:

(1)

CURRENCY:
Dollar
US$1 = £0.66
£1 = $1.51

The problem, it seems, is the cyclical nature of history. South Beach is hot again. The upscale crowd is moving back. High-fashion models, photographers, and movie stars share the clubs with shoestring travelers, creating quite an international meeting place. And you are never more than a few blocks from the beach. The prices have yet to soar, but they will. Try to check out South Beach before it leaves budget travelers behind. There is more to Miami than South Beach, but you can explore that next time.

One thing Miami Beach is not is a quiet resort town. Nor does it From resemble any other city in Florida. There is hedonism at its finest, 24 *Miami* hours a day, 7 days a week. The nightlife starts at midnight, and the after-hours clubs don't open until 5am. Pick up a copy of *New Times* or *Postmortem* to get the scoop on the local club scene, which is constantly changing. Many of the newer chic clubs are centered around Fifth or Sixth Streets and Washington. As a rule, things are less expensive and less touristy a block or so off of Ocean Drive. **The News Café** at [800 Ocean Drive ☎ (305) 531 0392] is where people stop at dawn for a bite to eat on their way home. In fact, this outdoor café is a hub for socializing all day long.

During the daytime, the action is centered on the beach, where people-watching is always in style. The area between Eighth and Twelfth Streets is a good place to meet the locals. To get a feel for the layout of SoBe, walk confidently through the lobby of the **Park Central Hotel** [640 Ocean Drive, ☎ (305) 538 1611], and catch the elevator up to the rooftop sun deck. The view of the Miami skyline and beaches is fabulous, and the Deco design of the restored hotel is easy on the eyes as well.

CHEAP SLEEPS

The Art Deco district is home to a multitude of hostels and budget hotel options.

Clay Hotel / Hostelling International Miami Beach

1438 Washington Avenue at Espanola Way
Miami Beach, FL 33139 USA
☎ (800) 379 CLAY, (305) 534 2988

This beautiful Deco hotel houses a fun hostel with a very international clientele. Facilities include laundry, kitchen, and a ride board. Private double rooms for $30. Beds in a quad go for $12, for members $10. No curfew, $5 key deposit.

Tropics

1550 Collins Avenue
Miami Beach, FL 33139 USA
☎ (305) 531 0361
Fax 305/ 531 8676

Tacky fliers proclaim a "clublike atmosphere," but it has a freshwater swimming pool ("with Poolbar") and our Miami researcher swears by it. Private rooms for $40 or hostel beds for $14. No curfew.

Miami Beach International Travelers Hostel

236 Ninth Street at Washington Avenue

Miami Beach, FL 33139 USA

☎ (305) 534 0268

Fax 305/ 534 5862

Mellow, fun place with a very international clientele. Features laundry, kitchen, the all-important common room with TV and a library, and an outdoor terrace. No curfew. Private rooms for $40 for one or two people, or $14 for a bed in a quad.

CHEAP EATS

For really cheap food, check out the bakeries and fruit stands, or grab something to take to the beach from **Tommy's Sandwiches**, at 1448A Washington Avenue.

At 7th and Collins, **Puerto Sagua** [☎ (305) 673 1115] offers good Cuban food in a family run restaurant. Don't leave Miami without trying out the subtly spiced Cuban cuisine.

Feel the need to multi-task? While eating at this Thai outdoor café and restaurant, you can also be shopping at its in-house crafts shop. **World Resources** is the name of the place, and it is located at 719 Lincoln Road [☎ (305) 534 9095]. Entrees average about $8.

TO & FROM THE AIRPORT

Miami International Airport [☎ (305) 876 7000] boasts facilities that make other airports look downright unfriendly. Stuck at the airport for a few hours? Work out those built-up aggressions at the little-known **Airport Health Club** [☎ (305) 871 4100], on the eighth floor of the airport's hotel, in Concourse E. Open 6am to 10pm daily. Use of their jogging path, weight room, swimming pool and Jacuzzi will set you back a mere $5. Afterwards, check out the Miami skyline from the Top of the Port Lounge, on the same floor. Weekdays from 5pm to 7pm, they have free hors d'oeuvres, and $1 beers if you ask for the Happy Hour Special. Sometimes they even have live music in the early evening.

For those of you who decide to leave this incredible airport in spite of all it has to offer, the "J" (East) Metro bus runs every 20 to 30 minutes to Miami Beach. Transfer there to the "C" or "K" buses south to South Beach. Fare is $1. To catch the bus from any concourse, proceed downstairs and across the street to the bus loop. SuperShuttle also offers service to South Beach for $14; call (305) 871 2000 or walk out the door near baggage claim and look for their yellow T-shirted representatives. Parking in South Beach is a nightmare, so cars are not advised.

UNIQUELY MIAMI

Buy mosquito repellent, rent a car (don't pay more than $30 a day; check at your hostel for discounts and car sharing ideas) and drive 30 minutes along Route 41 to **Shark Valley**, part of the Everglades National Park. Shark Valley is by no means tourist-free, but it is absolutely worth visiting. You can rent a bicycle for $2 an hour, and ride through the exotic, wildlife-filled, 22-mile loop. This is one of the best (and certainly the cheapest) ways to get a taste of the Everglades. Couch potatoes, there is also a tram tour available. And for the highly adventurous, contact the **Visitors' Center** [☎ (305) 242 7700] for advice, trail maps, and canoe or hiking tours. Remember: don't feed the alligators.

Council Travel

One Datran Center, Suite 220

9100 South Dadeland Boulevard

Miami, FL 33156 USA

☎ (800) 2COUNCIL, (305) 670 9261

Fax 305/ 670 9266

Internet: http://www.ciee.org/cts/ctshome.htm

Times to Call: 9:30am to 5:30pm

Type of Provider: Discount travel agent

Areas of Specialty: Worldwide

DESTINATIONS	SAMPLE ROUND-TRIP FARE	FULL COACH FARE
Amsterdam	$778	$948
Bangkok	$929	n/a
Frankfurt	$649	$898
Hong Kong	$825	n/a
London	$538	$766
Singapore	$1,129	n/a
Sydney	$1,408	n/a
Tokyo	$885	$1,690

Payment Methods: Cash, money order, personal check, Visa, MasterCard

In Business Since: 1947

(See the Council Travel listing on page 29 in the Chicago chapter for company background.)

East West Express

PO Box 30849

JFK Airport Station

Jamaica, NY 11430 USA

☎ (718) 656 6246

Contact: Tracy

Times to Call: 9am to 5pm

Type of Provider: Courier company

Areas of Specialty: Worldwide

DESTINATIONS	SAMPLE ROUND-TRIP FARE	FULL COACH FARE	LENGTH OF STAY
Melbourne	tba		
Sydney	tba		

Payment Methods: Cash, money order, personal check
Courier Duties on Return Trip: Yes
Minimum Age: 18 years
In Business Since: 1989
Recommended Advance Reservations: 2 months

Call to check on last-minute discounts. Couriers do not earn frequent-flyer miles, but can make date changes without penalty.

Halbart Express

7331 NW 35th Street
Miami, FL 33122 USA
☎ (305) 593 0260
Fax 305/ 593 0158
Contact: Ileana

Times to Call: 10am to 3pm
(Informational recording available after hours.)
Type of Provider: Courier company
Areas of Specialty: Worldwide

DESTINATIONS	SAMPLE ROUND-TRIP FARE	FULL COACH FARE	LENGTH OF STAY
London	$350	$766	7 days
Rio / Sao Paulo	$350	$1,450	7 to 30 days

Deposit: $100
Payment Methods: Cash, money order, personal check
Courier Duties on Return Trip: Yes
Minimum Age: 18 years
In Business Since: 1980
Recommended Advance Reservations: 1 to 3 months

Call to check on last-minute discounts. This company maintains a cancellation phone list. Fares increase by about $100 near Thanksgiving, Christmas, and July to August. Departure taxes are extra. By paying a $50 fee, couriers can extend their stays in London. Frequent-flyer miles accrue on these routes.

International Bonded Couriers (IBC)

8401 NW 17th Street

Miami, FL 33126 USA

☎ (305) 591 8080 or (305) 597 5331

Fax 305/ 591 2056

Contact: Carolina

Times to Call: 8am to 4pm

Type of Provider: Courier company

Areas of Specialty: Worldwide

DESTINATIONS	SAMPLE ROUND-TRIP FARE	FULL COACH FARE	LENGTH OF STAY
Buenos Aires	$400	$1,481	1 week

Deposit: $500!

Payment Methods: Cash, money order, personal check

Courier Duties on Return Trip: Yes

Minimum Age: 21 years

In Business Since: 1988

Recommended Advance Reservations: 2 months for Latin America, 2 weeks for the Caribbean

Luggage: One piece of carry-on only

Additional offices in Chicago, Los Angeles and New York. IBC keeps a cancellation phone list for you last-minute types. Flights to Freeport (Bahamas), Kingston (Jamaica), and Santo Domingo (Dominican Republic) are also regularly available. Fares are negotiated on a case by case basis, and must be booked several weeks in advance.

International Business Couriers

103 St. Vincent Street

Port of Spain, Trinidad

☎ (809) 623 4231 or 624 0445

Fax 809/ 623 4661

Contact: Lisa Ramsaran

Times to Call: 9am to 5pm

Type of Provider: Courier company

Areas of Specialty: Caribbean

DESTINATIONS	SAMPLE ROUND-TRIP FARE	FULL COACH FARE	LENGTH OF STAY	*From*
Port of Spain	$140	$774	varies	*Miami*

Deposit: None
Payment Methods: Cash, money order, personal check
Courier Duties on Return Trip: Yes
Minimum Age: 21 years
In Business Since: 1988
Recommended Advance Reservations: Several weeks
Luggage: One piece of carry-on only

Interworld Travel

800 Douglas Road, Suite 140
Coral Gables, FL 33134 USA
☎ (305) 443 4929
Fax 305/ 443 0351

Times to Call: 9am to 6pm
Type of Provider: Consolidator
Areas of Specialty: Europe and Africa

DESTINATIONS	SAMPLE ROUND-TRIP FARE	FULL COACH FARE
Amsterdam	$570	$948
Athens	$695	n/a
Frankfurt	$595	$898
Johannesburg	$1,395	$2,349
London	$440	$766
Nairobi	$1,295	n/a
Paris	$570	$858

Payment Methods: Cash, personal check, American Express
In Business Since: 1984

Good source of cheap airfares for the entire southeastern United States, and some flights from anywhere in the United States. The Johannesburg flight is particularly popular because it is direct. The brothers who own Interworld learned the business by working for years in several London bucket shops.

Lima Service

6115 Johnson Street
Hollywood, FL 33024 USA
☎ (954) 964 8400
Fax 954/ 964 0700
Contact: Elva or Gladys

Times to Call: 9am to 5pm
Type of Provider: Courier company
Areas of Specialty: Lima

DESTINATIONS	SAMPLE ROUND-TRIP FARE	FULL COACH FARE	LENGTH OF STAY
Lima	$430	$599	up to 30 days

Deposit: None
Payment Methods: Cash, money order, certified check
Minimum Age: 21
In Business Since: 1992
Recommended Advance Reservations: 4 to 6 weeks
Luggage: Carry-on only

Couriers carry no documents, but they give up their checked baggage space, which is used to ship apparel. The office staff speaks very little English, so it is useful to speak Spanish.

Line Haul Services

7859 NW 15th Street
Miami, FL 33126 USA
☎ (305) 477 0651
Fax 305/ 477 0659
Contact: Ileana or Zimri

Times to Call: 9am to 5pm
Type of Provider: Courier company
Areas of Specialty: Worldwide

DESTINATIONS	SAMPLE ROUND-TRIP FARE	FULL COACH FARE	LENGTH OF STAY
Buenos Aires	$500	$1,481	7 to 21 days
Caracas	$167	$310	7 to 21 days
Guatemala City	$217	$503	7 to 21 days
Guayaquil	$217	$780	7 to 21 days

La Paz	$417	$832	7 to 21 days	*From*
Lima	$217	$599	7 to 21 days	*Miami*
Madrid	$367	$1,250	7 days	
Managua	$217	$530	7 to 21 days	
Panama City	$217	$480	7 days	
Quito	$237	$778	7 to 21 days	
Rio de Janeiro	$467	$1,450	7 to 21 days	
San Salvador	$280	$622	7 days	
Sao Paulo	$467	$1,450	7 to 21 days	

Payment Methods: Cash, money order, personal check

Courier Duties on Return Trip: Yes

Minimum Age: 18 years

In Business Since: 1989

Recommended Advance Reservations: 2 months

Call to check on last-minute discounts. Flights for Panama City and San Salvador depart only once a week, on Sundays.

Martillo Express

1520 West 41st Street

Hialeah, FL 33012 USA

☎ (305) 822 0880

Fax 305/ 558 5890

Contact: Ana Louisa

Times to Call: 12pm to 5pm

Type of Provider: Courier company

Areas of Specialty: Worldwide

DESTINATIONS	SAMPLE ROUND-TRIP FARE	FULL COACH FARE	LENGTH OF STAY
Guayaquil	$200	$770	3 to 60 days
Quito	$200	$778	3 to 60 days

Payment Methods: Cash, money order, certified check

Courier Duties on Return Trip: Yes

Minimum Age: 18 years

In Business Since: 1989

Recommended Advance Reservations: 2 months

Call to check on last-minute discounts. This company maintains a

cancellation phone list. Flights may be discontinued during the summer of 1996, but are scheduled to restart in September.

STA Travel

3115 Commodore Plaza
Miami, FL 33133 USA
☎ (800) 777 0112, (305) 461 3444
Fax 305/ 461 4772
Internet: http://www.sta-travel.com/

Times to Call: 10am to 6pm
Type of Provider: Discount travel agency
Areas of Specialty: Worldwide

DESTINATIONS	SAMPLE ROUND-TRIP FARE	FULL COACH FARE
Amsterdam	$580	$948
Bangkok	$925	n/a
Frankfurt	$565	$898
London	$495	$766
Singapore	$945	n/a

Payment Methods: Cash, money order, certified check, personal
check, Visa, MasterCard, American Express
In Business Since: 1975

STA is the world's largest travel organization for students and young,
independent travelers. They have 120 locations worldwide. Some of
their best fares require student ID or carry a maximum age.

Their tickets are highly flexible, usually good for one year, and require
no advance purchase. Date changes can be made at any office worldwide for $25; refunds cost only $75. Such flexible tickets are a wise
choice for travelers going on long trips without fully concrete itineraries. STA tickets are priced based on one-way tickets, which makes
it easy to book open-jaw flights.

TFI Tours (Miami Travel Center)

2124 NE 123rd Street

Miami, FL 33181 USA

☎ (800) 745 8000, (305) 895 8115

Fax 305/ 895 4653

Times to Call: 9am to 6:30pm weekdays, 9am to 3pm Saturday

Type of Provider: Consolidator

Areas of Specialty: Europe, some Africa and Asia

DESTINATIONS	SAMPLE ROUND-TRIP FARE	FULL COACH FARE
Frankfurt	$600	$898
London	$530	$766
New York	$158	$437
Paris	$570	$858
Rome	$610	$958

Payment Methods: Cash, money order, certified check, Visa, MasterCard, American Express, Discover

In Business Since: 1982

TFI consolidates for 60 different airlines, including most of the major U.S. carriers. They sell to travel agents as well as the public.

Trans Air Systems

7264 NW 25th Street

Miami, FL 33122 USA

☎ (305) 592 1771

Fax 305/ 592 2927

Contact: Gloria

Times to Call: 9am to 5pm

Type of Provider: Courier company

Areas of Specialty: Worldwide

DESTINATIONS	SAMPLE ROUND-TRIP FARE	FULL COACH FARE	LENGTH OF STAY
Buenos Aires	$460	$1,481	up to 30 days
Guatemala City	$230	$503	up to 30 days
Mendoza	$460	n/a	up to 30 days
Montevideo	$460	$1,481	up to 30 days
Quito	$250	$778	up to 30 days
Santiago	$450	$1,481	up to 30 days

Payment Methods: Cash, money order, personal check

Courier Duties on Return Trip: Yes

Minimum Age: 18 years

In Business Since: 1989

Recommended Advance Reservations: 2 months

Call to check on last-minute discounts. This company maintains a cancellation phone list. These rates include departure tax. At a higher rate, Quito flights can be extended for up to one year.

NEW YORK, USA

MARKET TRENDS

Tremendous air traffic volume, along with hordes of consolidators and courier companies, make New York a great place to catch a budget flight. The best deals are on flights to Europe. Many of the domestic low-fare airlines serve New York, so it can be a good base from which to see the United States. However, real estate is pricey in the Big Apple, so expect higher-than-average prices for accommodations and food. Most foreign tourists need an onward ticket to get into the United States.

STOPPING OVER IN NEW YORK

New York is a fast-moving, exhilarating, at times overwhelming city. There is so much to do here, it is hard to know where to start. Clearly "dinner and a movie" is out—you can do that back at home. You might catch a Broadway play, if you can find tickets. If not, there's always off-Broadway, and even off-off-Broadway, where you sit close enough to touch the costumes of the talented performers. Maybe the free summer concerts by the Juilliard School (see below) are more your style, or the latest exhibit at SoHo's Alternative Museum, or the roller-rink disco near the Central Park Bandshell. The point is, you've got options. Pick up a copy of the *Village Voice* for the week's calendar of events.

By New York, we are really referring to Manhattan. The other boroughs each have a charm of their own. Nonetheless, for a brief visit, Manhattan is the place to be. Huge concrete structures bob like big apples in a frenzy of maniacal cabbies, well-tailored stockbrokers, gaunt-faced poets and fast-moving watch salesmen.

In the early 1990's, a well-publicized study ranked New York as the second most hostile city in the United States. Far from protesting their newly earned label, New Yorkers were furious that they finished second to Philadelphia! That's not to say that you shouldn't visit New York, but there are a few things you should be aware of. New Yorkers walk fast, talk fast, and boy, you better not get in their way on an escalator. You have to be streetwise to survive here. New Yorkers may have a reputation for being rude, but they've really just learned to keep their guards up all the time. Do the same, and you will do fine.

Yet while New York can be rough, it can also be romantic. Summer evenings are a great time to go out in New York. During July and August, musicians from the **Juilliard School** give free concerts in the sculpture garden at the **Museum of Modern Art** [14 West 54th Street near 5th Avenue, ☎ (212) 708 9491]. Doors open at 6pm, and the show starts at 8:30pm, Friday and Saturday only. Any time of year, you can catch the surprisingly romantic **Staten Island Ferry**. If you time it right, you get to see the sunset on the way out, and watch the lights come on in Manhattan on your way back. Bring a bottle of wine, and enjoy [take the #1 subway to South Ferry]. If you'd rather take a romantic stroll, walk across the **Brooklyn Bridge** at sunset [Catch the Lexington Line subway (4, 5 or 6) to City Hall].

Unlike most cities in the world, neighborhoods in New York change by the block. One minute you are walking in a decent neighborhood, and a moment later you find yourself in trouble. If this happens to you, just backtrack into a safer area. While it is difficult to judge the safety level of a place by its neighborhood, it is good to be able to orient yourself. The general layout goes like this: Midtown stretches from 23rd Street to 59th Street. Downtown is 23rd Street and below, Uptown is 59th Street and above. The East and West distinction tells you an address' location relative to Fifth Avenue and Central Park.

CHEAP SLEEPS

New York International Hostel (HI)
891 Amsterdam Avenue
New York, NY 10025
☎ (212) 932 2300

This is the largest hostel in the United States, with almost 500 beds. Located in a freshly remodeled landmark building, the hostel has kitchens and dining rooms, common lounges, and an outdoor garden. Open 24 hours, with no curfew. Beds are $20, plus $3 for non-members, $3 for sheets, and $2 for towels. Subway: 102nd Street. This Upper West Side spot books up fast, mainly with European travelers.

International House

Admissions Office

500 Riverside Drive

New York, NY 10027 USA

☎ (212) 316 8400

Fax 212/ 316 8415

The International House is a graduate dormitory run by a private foundation. It's on the Upper West Side, right next door to Columbia University with easy access to subways. Students, interns, visiting researchers and scholars are its target market, but student and even non-student travelers can take advantage of lower occupancy at International House in the spring, summer, and sometimes even Christmas holidays. The arrangements are Spartan but very secure. One added benefit is the Programs Office, which supplies not only tourist information but insider tips and sometimes freebie event tickets. Regular year residents are another source to find out about the "real" New York. Pay in cash or travelers' checks, or with Visa or MasterCard for bills of $50 or more. The current rate schedule is: 1 to 14 days at $25/day, 15 to 30 days at $18/day, 1 month at $14-18/day (depending on the room). Deluxe rooms are available at $60-90/ night, with air conditioning, cable television and private bathroom; these include large double beds and can accommodate four adults or even a small family.

Banana Bungalow

250 West 77th Street at Broadway

New York, NY 10024 USA

☎ (800) 6 HOSTEL, (212) 769 2441

Fax 212/ 877 5733

The same folks that brought you Los Angeles' most festive hostel have set up shop in the Big Apple. Look for more of the same friendly, social atmosphere and quality facilities here on the east side of Midtown. Features include a rooftop sun deck, common lounges, and kitchen facilities. Rates are $15-19 a night. For guaranteed reservations, fax ahead your credit card information, along with your name and arrival date.

Another way to avoid the pricey hotels and meet some New Yorkers at the same time is to book with **City Lights Bed and Breakfast**. Hosts tend to be normal New Yorkers who have an extra room or two. Many of them are in the arts, and can give you the scoop on the hottest happenings. Doubles start at $75 a night; unhosted apartments are also available. Call ☎ (212) 737 7049, or write to PO Box 20355, Cherokee Station, New York, NY 10028.

CHEAP EATS

You name the cuisine, they've got it in New York. Yet when push comes to shove, pizza and bagels define the budget food scene.

For bagels, there's no place like family run **Ess-A-Bagels** [359 First Avenue at 21st Street, ☎ (212) 260 2252]. This place still makes each bagel by hand, and boils them instead of steaming. The result is a proper bagel that's chewy on the inside, and crispy on the outside. Our reviewer said simply, "Amazing!" before falling into a blissful, self-indulgent trance. They have a second store on the east side of Midtown, at 831 Third Avenue and 50th Street [☎ (212) 980 1010].

Of all the pizzerias in Manhattan, which one is the real "Original Ray's?" The legal battles over the Ray's name rage on, and we don't want to touch them. Nonetheless, our anonymous sources point to **Famous Ray's**, at 465 Sixth Avenue and 11th Street, in the West Village [☎ (212) 243 2253]. You can order by the slice for $2.50. This Ray's uses only natural ingredients to produce a thick, cheesy pizza with a zesty sauce. Legend has it that two pizza-starved Americans studying in London found themselves compelled to fly to New York for a fix of Famous Ray's. They brought 40 pies back to London, and sold them at a profit to pay for their airfares!

For a real "come-as-you-are" kind of place in the East Village, check out **Dojo Restaurant** [24 St. Marks Place, between Second and Third, ☎ (212) 674 9821]. Don't let the tofu and stir-fry fool you— this place also cooks up a mean burger. Full dinners start at $2.95, and the most expensive meal on the menu is $8. They offer good music and outdoor tables to boot.

TO & FROM THE AIRPORT

From JFK, take the free Long Term Parking shuttle from any terminal to the Howard Beach subway station, where you catch the A train (Far Rockaway line). The subway takes you to Manhattan in about an hour, for about a buck.

From LaGuardia, catch the Q-33 bus to the end of the line (Roosevelt Avenue), where you can catch the subway into Manhattan. Each leg takes about 20 minutes, and costs $1.25 (coins only).

From Newark, take New Jersey Transit bus No. 62 (twice hourly from Terminals A, B and C; $1), or NJ Transit bus No. 300 Express (24-hour service, $7, runs every 15-30 minutes) for the 30-minute ride to Newark Penn Station. Then catch the PATH train to the World Trade Center in Manhattan ($1, 15-minute ride, operates 24 hours).

UNIQUELY NEW YORK

In the summertime, you'll find New Yorkers at **Shakespeare in the Park**. The New York Shakespeare Festival sponsors this free event at the open-air **Delacorte Theater** in Central Park. Call (212) 861 7277 for free tickets.

Tickets to tapings of **The Late Show with David Letterman** are much tougher to get, but where else can you get a better feel for New York's collective state of mind? Confirmed tickets must be requested by mail months in advance, but standby tickets are given out at noon each day at the box office of the Ed Sullivan Theater, 1697 Broadway between 53rd and 54th. Tapings start at 5:30pm.

Air Facility

153-40 Rockaway Boulevard

Jamaica, NY 11434 USA

☎ (718) 712 1769

Fax 718/ 712 1574

Contact: Alex or Marisa

Times to Call: 9am to 5pm

Type of Provider: Courier company

Areas of Specialty: Latin America and Europe

DESTINATIONS	SAMPLE ROUND-TRIP FARE	FULL COACH FARE	LENGTH OF STAY
Buenos Aires	$480	$1,493	7 to 13 days
Caracas	$210	$640	6, 9 or 14 days
Mexico City	$200	$687	6 to 9 days
Montevideo	$500	$1,693	7 to 15 days
Rio de Janeiro	$480	$1,683	7 to 14 days
Santiago	$480	$1,693	8 or 9 days
Sao Paulo	$480	$1,683	9 to 14 days

Payment Methods: Cash, money order, certified check

Courier Duties on Return Trip: Yes

Minimum Age: 18 years

In Business Since: 1985

Recommended Advance Reservations: 6 to 12 weeks

Call to check on last-minute discounts. This company maintains a cancellation phone list, but you must have traveled for Air Facility once in order to qualify for the list. Couriers earn frequent-flyer miles.

Air Facility maintains its own offices in the countries it serves. Other companies often contract with a local shipping company in each country, but Air Facility believes that its arrangement results in better service for clients and better treatment for couriers. When one of their couriers ran out of money during a bank closure in Caracas, the company actually loaned her money to help her through the crisis. They also keep a "blacklist" of unreliable couriers, so make sure you fulfill your obligations when you fly courier for them.

Bridges Worldwide

Building #197, JFK International Airport
Jamaica, NY 11430 USA
☎ (718) 244 7244
Fax 718/ 244 7240
Contact: Ruanda or Andrea

Times to Call: 9am to 5pm EST
Type of Provider: Courier company
Areas of Specialty: London

DESTINATIONS	SAMPLE ROUND-TRIP FARE	FULL COACH FARE	LENGTH OF STAY
London	$320	$446	1 to 6 weeks

Deposit: None
Payment Methods: Cash, personal check, Visa, MasterCard
Minimum Age: 21
In Business Since: 1992
Recommended Advance Reservations: 1 to 6 months
Luggage: Carry-on and 23kg of checked luggage

A cancellation phone list is available. Bridges is handling bookings for Virgin Express, so flights are on Virgin Atlantic.

Cheap Tickets, Inc.

1247 Third Avenue
New York, NY 10021 USA
☎ (800) 377 1000, (212) 570 1179
Fax 800/ 454 2555, (212) 906 1973

Times to Call: 9am to 5:30pm weekdays, 10am to 4:30pm Saturday
Type of Provider: Consolidator
Areas of Specialty: Hawaii, domestic USA, and international

DESTINATIONS	SAMPLE ROUND-TRIP FARE	FULL COACH FARE
Amsterdam	$339	$548
London	$349	$446
Los Angeles	$318	$883
Maui	$479	$2,164
Miami	$158	$460
Paris	$339	$758
Rome	$549	$818

Payment Methods: Cash, money order, certified check, personal check, Visa, MasterCard, American Express
In Business Since: 1986

Tickets are nonrefundable and non-changeable unless specifically noted by Cheap Tickets. Additional offices in Hawaii, Los Angeles, and San Francisco.

Council Travel

205 East 42nd Street
New York, NY 10017 USA
☎ (800) 2COUNCIL, (212) 822 2700
Fax 212/ 682 0129
Internet: http://www.ciee.org/cts/ctshome.htm

Times to Call: 9am to 5pm
Type of Provider: Discount travel agent
Areas of Specialty: Worldwide student, youth, and budget travel

DESTINATIONS	SAMPLE ROUND-TRIP FARE	FULL COACH FARE
Amsterdam	$456	$548
Bangkok	$929	$2,368
Hong Kong	$825	$1,846
London	$350	$446
Singapore	$1,006	$1,325
Sydney	$1,269	n/a
Tokyo	$839	$1,240

In Business Since: 1947
Payment Methods: Cash, money order, personal check, Visa, MasterCard

(See the Council Travel listing on page 29 in the Chicago chapter for company background.)

Courier Network

515 West 29th Street
New York, NY 10001 USA
☎ (212) 947 3738
Contact: Yossi

Times to Call: 6:30 to 8:30pm
Type of Provider: Courier company
Areas of Specialty: Israel

DESTINATIONS	SAMPLE ROUND-TRIP FARE	FULL COACH FARE	LENGTH OF STAY
Tel Aviv	$600	$1,362	2 to 60 days

Payment Methods: Cash, money order, personal check
Courier Duties on Return Trip: Yes
Minimum Age: 18 years
In Business Since: 1989
Recommended Advance Reservations: 2 to 4 months

One-way tickets are available. In the winter, you can book a flight as little as two months in advance. Prices increase all the way up to $800 in July and August. Flights are on TWA, and couriers do earn frequent-flyer miles. The flight out takes a day and a half, and the return flight takes a full day, so it is best to plan to stay in Israel as long as possible. Couriers may bring one checked bag plus a carry-on.

Discount Travel International (DTI)

169 West 81st Street
New York, NY 10024 USA
☎ (212) 362 3636
Fax 212/ 362 3236

Times to Call: 10am to 5:30pm
(Informational recording available after hours.)
Type of Provider: Standby and courier booking agent, consolidator
Areas of Specialty: Worldwide

DESTINATIONS	SAMPLE ROUND-TRIP FARE	FULL COACH FARE	LENGTH OF STAY
Courier flights:			
Bangkok	$599	$2,365	30 to 60 days
Buenos Aires	$520	$1,493	7 to 13 days

From New York			
Brussels	$375	$618	7 to 21 days
Caracas	$250	$640	6 to 14 days
Dublin	$299	$698	7 to 21 days
Hong Kong	$500	$1.846	up to 2 mos.
London	$325	$446	7 to 8 days
Mexico City	$250	$687	3 to 30 days
Milan	$375	$818	9 days
Montevideo	$520	$1,693	15 days
Rio de Janeiro	$525	$1,683	1 to 2 weeks
San Juan	$250	$450	3 to 30 days
Santiago	$520	$1,693	1 week
Singapore	$650	$1,325	7 to 30 days
Sydney	$600	n/a	up to 1 month

Consolidated fares:

Amsterdam	$399	$548
Buenos Aires	$650	$1,493
Cancun	$310	$640
Caracas	$525	$640
Chicago	$118	$305
Frankfurt	$399	$550
Los Angeles	$250	$883
Madrid	$389	$699
Miami	$150	$460
Paris	$399	$758
Rio de Janeiro	$650	$1,683
San Francisco	$250	$862

Deposit: $100 for courier flights
Payment Methods: Cash, money order, certified check, Visa, MasterCard
Courier Duties on Return Trip: Yes
Minimum Age: 18 years
In Business Since: 1989
Recommended Advance Reservations: 2 to 3 months for courier flights

One-way tickets are NOT available for courier flights. However, call to check on last-minute discounts on courier runs. DTI maintains a cancellation phone list. Some courier flights are on United Airlines, which permits couriers to check one bag. Ask about flights originating in Los

Angeles, Miami, or San Francisco. DTI gets new consolidator and space-available destinations all the time, so call them to get the latest details. Space-available is the single cheapest way for flexible travelers to fly within the USA. Currently, most of these flights are on World Airways and Tower Air.

From New York

East West Express

PO Box 30849
JFK Airport Station
Jamaica, NY 11430 USA
☎ (718) 656 6246
Contact: Tracy

Times to Call: 10:30am to 2:30pm
(Informational recording available after hours.)
Type of Provider: Courier company
Areas of Specialty: Worldwide

DESTINATIONS	SAMPLE ROUND-TRIP FARE	FULL COACH FARE	LENGTH OF STAY
Auckland	$1,050	n/a	up to 30 days
Bangkok	$650	$2,365	up to 90 days
Beijing	$750	$1,641	up to 90 days
Brisbane	$1,050	n/a	up to 90 days
Cairns	$1,050	n/a	up to 90 days
Hong Kong	$750	$1,846	up to 90 days
Jakarta	$1,000	n/a	up to 6 mos
Johannesburg	$1,000	$2,349	up to 45 days
Kuala Lumpur	$1,000	n/a	up to 6 mos
Manila	$1,000	n/a	up to 6 mos
Melbourne	$1,050	n/a	7 to 90 days
Seoul	$750	$1,565	up to 90 days
Sydney	$1,050	n/a	7 to 90 days
Taipei	$750	$1,412	up to 90 days
Tokyo	$750	$1,240	up to 90 days

Payment Methods: Cash, money order, personal check
Courier Duties on Return Trip: Yes
Minimum Age: 18 years
In Business Since: 1989
Recommended Advance Reservations: 2 months

From
New York

Call to check on last-minute discounts. Prices for reserved courier flights are a bit high, but the length of stay is exceptionally long.

Halbart Express

147-05 176th Street
Jamaica, NY 11434 USA
☎ (718) 656 5000
Fax 718/ 244 0559

Times to Call: 10am to 3pm
(Informational recording available after hours ☎ (718) 656 8189.)
Type of Provider: Courier company
Areas of Specialty: Worldwide

DESTINATIONS	SAMPLE ROUND-TRIP FARE	FULL COACH FARE	LENGTH OF STAY
Brussels	$328	$618	7 days
Copenhagen	$328	$1,318	1 week
Dublin	$378	$698	7 days
Frankfurt	$328	$550	8 days
Hong Kong	$528	$1,846	14 days
London	$278	$446	7 days
Madrid	$378	$699	8 days
Milan	$378	$818	14 days
Paris	$378	$758	1 week
Rome	$378	$818	8 days
Seoul	$528	$1,565	14 days
Singapore	$528	$1,325	14 days
Stockholm	$378	$1,318	7 days
Tokyo	$528	$1,240	14 days
Zurich	$378	$1,368	7 days

Deposit: $100
Payment Methods: Cash, money order, personal check
Courier Duties on Return Trip: Yes
Minimum Age: 18 years
In Business Since: 1980
Recommended Advance Reservations: 1 to 3 months

Call to check on last-minute discounts. This company maintains a cancellation phone list. Frequent-flyer miles accrue.

Couriers must meet at the office in Jamaica, New York two hours prior to departure. By subway, get off the F line at Parsons Boulevard, then catch the Q-113 bus to the Halbart office. The Halbart driver brings the courier and the mailbags to the airport.

Fares increase by about $100 near Thanksgiving, Christmas, and July through August.

Jupiter Air (Micom America)

Building No. 14
JFK International Airport
Jamaica, New York 11430 USA
☎ (718) 656 6050
Fax 718/ 656 7263
Contact: Dania or Lisa

Times to Call: 10am to 3pm only
Type of Provider: Courier company
Areas of Specialty: Worldwide

DESTINATIONS	SAMPLE ROUND-TRIP FARE	FULL COACH FARE	LENGTH OF STAY
Hong Kong	$500	$1,846	7 to 30 days
London	$325	$446	7 to 30 days
Singapore	$550	$1,325	10 to 30 days

Annual Fee: $35 for 3 years
Deposit: $100
Payment Methods: Cash, money order, certified check, personal check
Courier Duties on Return Trip: Yes
Minimum Age: 18 years
In Business Since: 1988
Recommended Advance Reservations: 0 to 3 months
Luggage: United Airlines flights allow only two checked bags.

Ask about last-minute discounts and the cancellation phone list.

Hong Kong is Jupiter Air's hub city. Thus it is sometimes possible to reserve a courier flight from Hong Kong to other Asian cities, such as Bangkok or Tokyo. Keep in mind that you must be back in Hong Kong in time for your return flight to the US. The Hong Kong run includes one free night in a Tokyo hotel.

Additional offices in Hong Kong, Los Angeles, London, San Francisco, Seoul, Sydney, Taipei, and Tokyo. Jupiter strongly favors repeat business. Last-minute flights can be had for 50 percent off.

New Frontiers

12 East 33rd Street

New York, NY 10016 USA

☎ (800) 366 6387, (212) 779 0600

Fax 212/ 779 1006

Internet: http://www.sv.vtcom.fr/nf/ (note: French language site)

Times to Call: 9am to 7pm weekdays, 10am to 4pm Saturday

Type of Provider: Consolidator and charter operator

Areas of Specialty: Worldwide

DESTINATIONS	SAMPLE ROUND-TRIP FARE	FULL COACH FARE
London	$398	$446
Marseilles / Nice	$558	$1,418
Milan	$638	$818
Paris	$438	$758
Rome	$658	$818

Payment Methods: Cash, money order, certified check, Visa, MasterCard, American Express

In Business Since: 1967

Discount tickets on Tower Air, American Trans Air, Continental, KLM, American Airlines, and CORSAIR. Started in 1967 by a French law student who was putting together a trip to Morocco for some friends, the entire trip cost a quarter of the price of a round-trip air ticket from Paris to Casablanca. Later, he organized a second trip for 300 people, and Nouvelles Frontières (as the company is known in Europe) was born. They now have 132 offices worldwide, and some of the cheapest flights to or from the French-speaking world.

New Frontiers fought the airline cartel in a landmark 1985 case before the European Court of Justice, and won the right to sell discounted airfares.

Now Voyager

74 Varick Street, Suite 307
New York, NY 10013 USA
☎ (212) 431 1616
Fax 212/ 334 5243, or 219 1753

Times to Call: 10am to 5:30pm weekdays, 12pm to 4:30pm Saturday
(Informational recording available from 6pm to 10am.)
Type of Provider: Courier broker, charter operator and standby broker
Areas of Specialty: Worldwide

DESTINATIONS	SAMPLE ROUND-TRIP FARE	FULL COACH FARE	LENGTH OF STAY
Aukland	$1,049	n/a	up to 90 days
Bangkok	$689	$2,365	up to 90 days
Beijing	$589	$1,641	up to 90 days
Buenos Aires	$499	$1,493	7, 8 or 13 days
Caracas	$220	$640	6 to 9 days
Copenhagen	$388	$1,318	1 week
Dublin	$399	$698	7 or 8 days
Frankfurt	$388	$550	1 week
Hong Kong	$699	$1,846	up to 90 days
Johannesburg	$999	$2,349	up to 45 days
London	$335	$446	7 to 30 days
Madrid	$399	$699	7 to 15 days
Manila	$799	n/a	2 weeks
Mexico City	$169	$687	varies
Milan	$438	$818	varies
Montevideo	$499	$1,693	varies
Paris	$438	$758	1 week
Rio de Janeiro	$550	$1,683	varies
Rome	$438	$818	8 or 14 days
San Juan, PR	$259	$450	3 to 30 days
Santiago	$499	$1,693	6 to 9 days
Sao Paulo	$510	$1,683	varies
Seoul	$589	$1,565	up to 90 days
Singapore	$589	$1,325	up to 90 days
Stockholm	$388	$1,318	1 week
Sydney	$1,099	n/a	up to 90 days
Taipei	$589	$1,412	up to 90 days
Tokyo	$689	$1,368	up to 90 days

Annual Fee: $50

Deposit: $100

Payment Methods: Cash, money order, certified check, personal check, Visa, MasterCard, American Express

Courier Duties on Return Trip: Yes

Minimum Age: 18 years

In Business Since: 1984

Recommended Advance Reservations: 1 to 3 months

Call to check on last-minute discounts. A consolidator fare is available to Amsterdam for $499. Ask about the last-minute phone list, called the Jet-Setters Roster. They claim that 95 percent of standby customers get onto their first flight.

Omega World Travel

875 Third Avenue, Mezz.

New York, NY 10022 USA

☎ (800) 545 1003, (212) 753 4900

Fax 212/ 753 0673

Times to Call: 9am to 5:30pm

Type of Provider: Discount travel agent

Areas of Specialty: Europe, Middle East, domestic USA

Payment Methods: For TWA deal, accepts credit cards only.

In Business Since: 1970

By knowing to ask for the "TWA Global Discount fares," you will automatically get 20 percent off all domestic TWA fares, and 25 percent off all international fares. You get the same seat on the same flight—you just pay less. Call TWA first at ☎ (800) 221 2000 to get the flight number and lowest published fare for the flight you want, then call Omega World Travel to book the ticket. Senior and student fares are excluded from this offer. How do they do it? Under its restructuring plan, TWA owes investor Carl Icahn roughly $600 million. Carl has the right to buy TWA tickets at 40 percent or more off of published fares. He marks them up a bit and resells them, with the profit going to reduce TWA's debt. Omega buys from Carl's agent, and passes the 20 to 25 percent discount on to you. This deal will continue until the debt is paid in full, which will probably be in 1998 or later.

We list additional Omega offices in the Chicago, Los Angeles, and San Francisco chapters. Not near one of these cities? No problem. Omega has 280 offices nationwide. Call (800) 955 2582 to find the office nearest you.

Rush Courier, Inc.

481 49th Street

Brooklyn, NY 11220 USA

☎ (718) 439 8181

Fax 718/ 439 9043

Contact: Eileen Martinez

Times to Call: 1-4pm

Type of Provider: Courier company

Areas of Specialty: Puerto Rico

DESTINATIONS	SAMPLE ROUND-TRIP FARE	FULL COACH FARE	LENGTH OF STAY
San Juan	$225	$450	3 to 30 days

Payment Methods: Cash, money order, personal check

Courier Duties on Return Trip: Yes

Minimum Age: 18 years

In Business Since: 1987

Recommended Advance Reservations: 2 to 3 months

One-way tickets to San Juan cost $150. Rush imposes a $25 cancellation fee. Call to check on last-minute discounts. This company maintains a cancellation phone list. Couriers are permitted two carry-ons only. Couriers earn frequent-flyer miles.

STA Travel

10 Downing Street (Sixth Avenue & Bleecker)

New York, NY 10014 USA

☎ (800) 777 0112, (212) 627 3111

Fax 212/ 477 7348

Internet: http://www.sta-travel.com/

Times to Call: 10am to 6pm

Type of Provider: Discount travel agency

Areas of Specialty: Worldwide

DESTINATIONS	SAMPLE ROUND-TRIP FARE	FULL COACH FARE
Amsterdam	$475	$548
Bangkok	$1,090	$2,365
Frankfurt	$525	$550
Hong Kong	$990	$1,846
London	$400	$446
Singapore	$1,100	$1,325
Sydney	$1,375	n/a
Tokyo	$795	$1,240

Payment Methods: Cash, money order, certified check, personal check, Visa, MasterCard, American Express

In Business Since: 1975

STA is the world's largest travel organization for students and young, independent travelers. They have 120 locations worldwide. Some of their best fares require student ID, or carry a maximum age.

Their tickets are highly flexible, usually good for one year, and require no advance purchase. Date changes can be made at any office world-wide for $25; refunds cost only $75. Such flexible tickets are a wise choice for travelers going on long trips without fully concrete itineraries. STA tickets are priced based on one-way tickets, which makes it easy to book open-jaw flights.

TFI Tours

34 West 32nd Street

New York, NY 10001 USA

☎ (800) 745 8000, (212) 736 1140

Fax 212/ 564 4081

Type of Provider: Consolidator

Areas of Specialty: Worldwide

DESTINATIONS	SAMPLE ROUND-TRIP FARE	FULL COACH FARE
Amsterdam	$300	$548
Frankfurt	$380	$550
Johannesburg	$1,024	$2,349
London	$370	$446
Miami	$158	$460
Paris	$380	$758
Rio de Janeiro	$800	$1,683
Tokyo	$838	$1,240

Payment Methods: Cash, money order, certified check, Visa, MasterCard, American Express, Discover

In Business Since: 1982

TFI consolidates for 60 different airlines, including most of the major U.S. carriers. They sell to travel agents as well as the public.

Travac

989 Sixth Avenue

New York, NY 10018 USA

☎ (800) 872 8800, (212) 563 3303

Times to Call: 8:30am to 8:30pm

Type of Provider: Nationwide consolidator

Areas of Specialty: Europe

DESTINATIONS	SAMPLE ROUND-TRIP FARE	FULL COACH FARE
Atlanta to Amsterdam	$620	$1,388
Miami to Amsterdam	$690	$948
Miami to Paris	$580	$858
New York to Paris	$530	$758
San Francisco to Frankfurt	$780	$1,558
San Francisco to London	$670	$1,158
San Francisco to Moscow	$960	$1,778

Payment Methods: Cash, money order, certified check, Visa, MasterCard

In Business Since: 1979

Consolidates for major airlines like Delta and Air France.

World Courier

1313 Fourth Avenue

New Hyde Park, NY 11040 USA

☎ (516) 354 2600

Contact: Barbara Whitting

Times to Call: 9am to 5pm

Type of Provider: Courier company

Areas of Specialty: Worldwide

DESTINATIONS	SAMPLE ROUND-TRIP FARE	FULL COACH FARE	LENGTH OF STAY
Mexico City	$200	$687	3 to 30 days
Milan	$300	$818	9 days

Payment Methods: Cash, money order, personal check

Courier Duties on Return Trip: No

Minimum Age: 18 years

In Business Since: 1980

Recommended Advance Reservations: 2 months

World prefers to use New York area residents, and couriers must hold a U.S. or EC passport. Couriers are allowed one piece of checked luggage on most flights. For the Milan flight, couriers get one checked bag but zero carry-ons.

The screening process at World is tougher than average. Call to request an application. Because their niche is premium courier services, they have to be very selective about whom they use to accompany their documents. In fact, they have been talking about using in-house couriers only, so PLEASE do follow your instructions carefully if you fly for them.

World has a great cancellation phone list, but you must have flown with them before in order to get on it. At the last minute, you fly for free, and they pay the first night's hotel at your destination.

SAN FRANCISCO, USA

CHAPTER 7

MARKET TRENDS

San Francisco is a good jumping-off point for travel to the Pacific Rim. There is a healthy mix of discount, charter and courier flights to Asia and Australia, and plenty of discount and charter opportunities to Europe. Courier flights to Europe are few and far between—you may find an occasional flight to London, but you will have to book far in advance. San Francisco is one of the best places in the world to buy an around-the-world or circle-Pacific ticket. Some consolidators will also sell tickets by mail to travelers flying between international points other than San Francisco. Most foreign tourists need an onward ticket to get into the United States.

STOPPING OVER IN SAN FRANCISCO

Dock-sitting Otis Redding was not the only visitor to find himself enamored with the City by the Bay. Condé Nast Traveler readers recently named San Francisco the number one city destination in the world. This scenic city actually holds a beauty contest of sorts, doling out the limited amount of new building permits only to developers who submit the most eye-pleasing designs.

San Francisco is a patchwork of neighborhoods, from the post-hippie **Haight-Ashbury** to the yuppie **Pacific Heights** and the trendy, industrial club district **South of Market (SoMa)**. The key to understanding San Francisco is to explore it one neighborhood at a time. "The City," as it is known by locals, is compact—a brisk 30-minute walk will take you from the waterfront through **North Beach**, past **Chinatown**, the **Financial District**, and down to **Market Street**. The Muni bus and BART subway systems are cheap and convenient ways to get to the starting point for your walking adventures.

The center of the burgeoning San Francisco jazz scene is **Café du Nord**, at 2170 Market in the Castro [☎ (415) 861 5016]. The decor is upscale, yet the club draws a young, artsy crowd which is far too diverse (and far too hip) to categorize. Once a notorious speakeasy, du Nord now features some of the Bay Area's hottest jazz and blues acts, including rising star Lavay Smith and the Red Hot Skillet Lickers. Eat dinner there to get a cabaret table. More of a local secret is live

TELEPHONE COUNTRY CODE:
(1)
CURRENCY:
Dollar
US$1 = £0.66
£1 = $1.51

salsa on Tuesdays. The Fabulous Juan offers free salsa lessons for novices at 9pm. At 10pm the curtain goes up and the live band goes on stage. No partners necessary.

Avoid the T-shirt-shop-infested tourist trap that is Fisherman's Wharf at all costs. The only exception to this rule is Pier 43 1/2, which is where you catch the Red and White ferries. On weekends, try brunch at the social, outdoor tables of **Sam's Anchor Café** [27 Main St. across the Golden Gate in Tiburon, ☎ (415) 435 4527]. The views from the Tiburon waterfront are great, but for true drama, hike to the top of **Mount Tamalpais**. A less strenuous hike with pleasant views is the five-mile perimeter trail at **Angel Island State Park**. An oasis in the middle of the bay, Angel Island offers beaches, foraging deer, great picnic spots and historic buildings. Call the **Red and White Fleet** at (415) 546 2628 for more information and schedules for either destination.

CHEAP SLEEPS

The Globe Hostel
10 Hallam Place
San Francisco, CA 94103 USA
☎ (415) 431 0540
Fax 415/ 431 3286

A hip crowd and well-designed common areas make this hostel a fun place to stay. The staff points out the most interesting of the nearby SoMa clubs each night. The hostel serves breakfast and dinner, and features a sun roof, TV lounge, pool table, and a bar downstairs. Dorm rooms are $10-$15, private rooms $36. The Globe does not take credit cards. Weekends, wander over to China Basin for outdoor brunches on the waterfront. My favorite, **The Ramp**, is at 855 China Basin, near the south end of 4th Street [☎ (415) 621 2378]. Local yachtsmen sail up to the restaurant to eat. Play your cards right, and you might even talk your way aboard as an extra deckhand.

Green Tortoise Guest House
494 Broadway
San Francisco, CA 94133 USA
☎ (415) 834 9060
Fax 415/ 956 4900

The Green Tortoise Guest House's extremely central location makes it

a great place from which to explore the City. It's on the edge of North Beach and Chinatown, half an hour or less on foot from about anywhere. Don't let the occasional strip joint fool you—this is a safe, up-and-coming neighborhood, with great food, cafés, and drinking establishments. Capacity is 85 people. Custom bunk beds give you lots of space in the rooms. Great showers and a sauna add to the appeal. Dorm rooms $15, singles $20, doubles $35. No curfew. Run by the Green Tortoise alternative bus people. They will be opening a bar/café/upscale billiards hall below the hostel, and plan to offer drink discounts to hostellers.

The San Francisco International Hostel (HI / AYH)
Building 240, Fort Mason
San Francisco, CA 94123 USA
☎ (415) 771 7277

There are great views of the sun setting under the Golden Gate Bridge, and rumor has it that the produce section of the nearby **Marina Safeway** supermarket is a great place to initiate interesting romantic relationships. Don't expect to meet a lot of people at the hostel itself, though. For some reason, the place is very quiet, and fails to encourage interactions between travelers. But the views from Fort Mason are remarkable. At $13 a night, this place is a bargain. Call two days ahead and book with a credit card, this hostel is always full in the summertime. Lights out at midnight, and lockout at 2am.

The Red Victorian
1665 Haight Street
San Francisco, CA 94117 USA
☎ (415) 864 1978
Fax 415/ 863 3293

A casual, artistic and friendly atmosphere pervades this 18-room bed and breakfast, which is perched atop a family-style breakfast nook and meditative art gallery. Outside the door is the eclectic, young population of the Upper Haight, who come to check out the alternative music and clothing stores in the area. The Red Vic is the only inn we know of that gives guided tours of its elaborately and individually decorated bathrooms. Experience a 25-year time warp in the Summer of Love Room, or get cozy in the Teddy Bear Room. Rates start at $86 a night double, with shared bath. Continental breakfast in the Global Village is included. Don't miss the tapas and sangría at **Cha Cha Cha** [1801 Haight, ☎ (415) 386 5758], just down the block. Or sprawl out on the pillows and sample inexpensive Mediterranean food at **Kan Zaman** [1793 Haight, ☎ (415) 751 9656]. Smoking the exotic tobacco hookas is extra, but watching the belly dancers is free. For unlimited daytime recreation possibilities, **Golden Gate Park** is but a short walk away. Clearly, the Red Vic has chosen an interesting neighborhood.

CHEAP EATS

There are lots of great Asian restaurants in Chinatown, where a meal will set you back only $3 to $5. One good bet is **Sam Woh's**, at 813 Washington [☎ (415) 982 0596]. Pop into **Wee On Co. Market**, directly across the street, if you fancy beer or wine with your dinner. Because the only beverage served at Sam Woh's is tea, jaywalking to Wee On has become a tradition.

For only a dollar more a plate, **House of Nanking's** spicy Chinese cuisine causes hour-long lines at lunch or dinner. Sizzling prawns and Nanking beef are quite popular, but Chef Fang does wonderful things even with humble chow mein [919 Kearny at Columbus, ☎ (415) 421 1429]. Visit them at off-peak hours, or break up into groups of two. *The Zagat Survey* rates them among the top 25 restaurants in San Francisco, yet the bill won't exceed $9 a person.

In the Mission, **La Cumbre** [☎ (415) 863 8205] at 515 Valencia and 16th serves up some of the city's best burritos for $3.50; while you're in the neighborhood, step over to 647 Valencia for unpretentious beer, pool and dancing at the **Elbo Room** [☎ (415) 552 7788].

North Beach Pizza is another local favorite, with locations at 1310 and 1499 Grant Avenue [☎ (415) 433 2444]. At the **Bocce Café**, mix and match a dozen pastas with a dozen sauces for $5.95 a plate, in a pleasantly candle-lit atmosphere. They are also in North Beach, at 478 Green, near Grant [☎ (415) 981 2044].

TO & FROM THE AIRPORT

Take a shuttle bus from SFO airport to your doorstep (or vice-versa) for about $11; try SuperShuttle at [☎ (415) 558 8500]. By bus, the

SamTrans 7B and 7F buses [☎ (800) 660 4287] depart from the

SamTrans sign on the upper level every 30 minutes. Forty minutes and exactly $0.85 later ($2 for the 7F, on which large luggage is not allowed), you arrive at the downtown Transbay Terminal at First and Mission. From there you can catch a connecting Muni bus to anywhere in San Francisco.

UNIQUELY SAN FRANCISCO

Skip Fisherman's Wharf and Pier 39. Instead, catch a cable car (the Powell-Hyde line from Powell and Market Streets). Hop off at curvaceous **Lombard Street**, where you will enjoy a fabulous view of the City (when the fog is at bay). Then wander down Lombard to **Columbus Street**, where you can explore the old Italian neighborhood of North Beach. Follow the swirling aromas of garlic and espresso—Bohemian cafés, shops and eateries abound. Turn right at the Transamerica Pyramid to explore **Chinatown**.

For a different sort of adventure, tour the **Castro**, the slightly upscale hangout of San Francisco's strong gay and lesbian communities. To get there, take the Muni west on Market Street to Castro. The area's cafés, jazz clubs, and leather shops attract bustling crowds. Follow Castro Street as it turns into Divisadero, then head west on Haight to explore the equally infamous **Haight Ashbury**, home of dive bars and counterculture youth. The hippies have migrated, but the area is still lively, especially on weekends. Check with the **Visitor's Bureau** [☎ (415) 391 2000] for the dates of the **Haight Street Fair** and the **Castro Street Fair**, two summer festivals that bring out roughly 100,000 people.

Air Brokers International

323 Geary Street, Suite 411

San Francisco, CA 94102 USA

☎ (800) 883 3273, (415) 397 1383

Fax 415/ 397 4767

Internet: airbrokr@aimnet.com, or http://www.aimnet.com/~airbrokr/

Times to Call: 9:15am to 5pm

Type of Provider: Consolidator

Areas of Specialty: Worldwide, especially around-the-world fares

DESTINATIONS	SAMPLE ROUND-TRIP FARE	FULL COACH FARE
Bali	$870	n/a
Bangkok	$720	$1,452
London	$500	$1,158
Paris	$500	$1,558
Sydney	$800	$1,408
Tel Aviv	$900	$1,650

Payment Methods: Cash, money order, certified check, personal check, Visa, MasterCard, American Express

In Business Since: 1985

Frequently consolidates for Garuda, as well as Air France, Thai, Malaysian, China Air, Cathay Pacific, Qantas, EVA Airways, and Philippine Air. Air Brokers now also consolidates for VASP, LACSA, and AeroPeru, making them a good option when you are seeking that bargain flight to South America. With 30 sister companies around the world, they are in a good position to ferret out those good deals anywhere in the world.

Still, Air Brokers' specialty is constructing circle-Pacific and around-the-world fares. For example, fly Los Angeles–Hong Kong–Bangkok–Bali–Hawaii–Los Angeles for $949; or New York–Hong Kong–Bangkok–Delhi–Amsterdam/London–New York for $1,399. And should you need to purchase a ticket from outside the USA, give them a call.

AVIA Travel

717 Market Street
San Francisco, CA 94103 USA
☎ (800) 950 2842, (415) 536 4155
Fax 415/ 536 4158
Internet: avia@igc.apc.org

Times to Call: 9am to 5pm
Type of Provider: Discount travel agency
Areas of Specialty: Africa, Asia and around-the-world

DESTINATIONS	SAMPLE ROUND-TRIP FARE	FULL COACH FARE
Bangkok	$761	$1,452
Hanoi/Ho Chi Minh	$1,000	n/a
Kathmandu	$1,271	n/a

Payment Methods: Cash, money order, certified check, Visa, MasterCard, American Express
In Business Since: 1986

AVIA's specialty is constructing circle-Pacific and around-the-world fares. For example, fly San Francisco–Hong Kong–Bangkok–Singapore–Jakarta–Bali–Hawaii–Los Angeles for $1,230; or San Francisco–Tokyo–Kuala Lumpur–Bangkok–Europe / London–San Francisco for $1,500.

Fax or write from abroad for exported discount tickets by mail. AVIA's focus on Asia enables them to get special deals on land packages as well. AVIA is owned by Volunteers In Asia, a private, nonprofit, non-sectarian organization dedicated to increased understanding between the United States and Asia. A percentage of AVIA's profits support the programs of Volunteers in Asia.

Bridges Worldwide / Virgin Express

Building #197, JFK International Airport
Jamaica, NY 11430 USA
☎ (718) 529 6814, then dial 8 for courier department
Fax 718/ 244 7240
Contact: Ruanda or Andrea

From	Times to Call: 9am to 5pm
San Francisco	Type of Provider: Courier company
	Areas of Specialty: Pacific Rim

DESTINATIONS	SAMPLE ROUND-TRIP FARE	FULL COACH FARE	LENGTH OF STAY
London	$440	$1,158	up to 6 weeks

Deposit: None
Payment Methods: Cash, checks, Visa, MasterCard, American Express
Courier Duties on Return Trip: Yes
Minimum Age: 21 years
In Business Since: 1992
Recommended Advance Reservations: 6 to 8 weeks
Luggage: Carry-on plus 23kg of checked luggage

Courier runs to Asia are expected soon. All flights are on Virgin Atlantic.

Buenaventura Travel

595 Market Street, 22nd Floor
San Francisco, CA 94105 USA
☎ (800) 286 8872, (415) 777 9777
Fax 415/ 777 9871

Times to Call: 9am to 5pm
Type of Provider: Consolidator
Areas of Specialty: Latin America

DESTINATIONS	SAMPLE ROUND-TRIP FARE	FULL COACH FARE
Buenos Aires	$899	n/a
Guatemala City	$570	$890
Lima	$780	n/a
Rio de Janeiro	$899	$1,794
San Jose	$570	$882
Santiago	$899	n/a

Payment Methods: Cash, money order, certified check, personal check, Visa, MasterCard, American Express
In Business Since: 1982

Prices are generally 15 to 20 percent off of APEX fares, often without the advance-purchase requirements that the airlines would impose. Most fares are "common rated" (same price) for departures from either San Francisco or Los Angeles.

These IATA, ARC and Better Business Bureau members consolidate for the "main national carriers" of Central and South America. For countries where visas are necessary, they provide visa assistance for free. This mom-and-pop operation provides very personalized service. They'll even give you advice and maps for various cities and expeditions.

Char-Tours

562 Mission Street, Suite 500
San Francisco, CA 94105 USA
☎ (800) 323 4444, (415) 495 8881
Fax 800/ 388 8838, 415/ 543 8010

Times to Call: 9am to 5pm
Type of Provider: Consolidator
Areas of Specialty: Europe and Middle East

DESTINATIONS	SAMPLE ROUND-TRIP FARE	FULL COACH FARE
Athens	$760	n/a
London	$555	$1,158
Milan	$695	$1,558
Moscow	$775	$1,778
Paris	$410	$1,558
Tel Aviv	$955	$1,650
Zurich	$675	$1,608

Payment Methods: Cash, personal check, Visa, MasterCard, American Express
In Business Since: 1957

Booking agents for New Frontiers' charter airline Corsair. Also consolidates for a variety of major scheduled airlines: Air Canada, Air France, Canadian Air, KLM, Northwest, United and others.

Char-Tours books departures from airports across the country, but all flights are booked through the toll-free number at the San Francisco address.

Offers a few flights to the Pacific Rim and to Latin America, but no domestic flights whatsoever.

Cheap Tickets, Inc.
1230 El Camino Real, Suite L
San Bruno, CA 94066 USA
☎ (800) 377 1000, (650) 588 3700
Fax 800/ 454 2555

Times to Call: 6am to 8pm weekdays, 9am to 3pm Saturday
Type of Provider: Consolidator
Areas of Specialty: Hawaii, domestic USA, and international

DESTINATIONS	SAMPLE ROUND-TRIP FARE	FULL COACH FARE
Bangkok	$889	$1,452
London	$630	$1,158
Maui	$309	$638
Paris	$779	$1,558
Sydney	$799	$1,408
Tokyo	$589	$930

Payment Methods: Cash, money order, certified check, personal check, Visa, MasterCard, American Express
In Business Since: 1986

Tickets are nonrefundable and non-changeable unless specifically noted by Cheap Tickets. Additional offices in Hawaii, Los Angeles, and New York.

Council Travel
530 Bush Street
San Francisco, CA 94108 USA
☎ (800) 2COUNCIL, (415) 421 3473
Fax 415/ 421 5603
Internet: http://www.ciee.org/cts/ctshome.htm

Times to Call: 9am to 5pm
Type of Provider: Discount travel agent
Areas of Specialty: Worldwide student, youth, and budget travel

DESTINATIONS	SAMPLE ROUND-TRIP FARE	FULL COACH FARE	*From*
Amsterdam	$576	$1,468	*San Francisco*
Bangkok	$765	$1,452	
Frankfurt	$529	$1,558	
Hong Kong	$679	$935	
London	$529	$1,158	
Singapore	$809	$1,080	
Sydney	$915	$1,408	
Tokyo	$529	$930	

Payment Methods: Cash, money order, personal check, Visa, MasterCard
In Business Since: 1947

Open from 10am to 2pm Saturdays for walk-in clients only.

(See the Council Travel listing on page 29 in the Chicago chapter for company background.)

Cut Throat Travel Outlet

737 Post Street, Suite 615
San Francisco, CA 94109 USA
☎ (800) 642 8747, (415) 981 8747
Fax 415/ 931 7327

Times to Call: 10am to 6pm
Type of Provider: Consolidator
Areas of Specialty: Worldwide

DESTINATIONS	SAMPLE ROUND-TRIP FARE	FULL COACH FARE
Bangkok	$699	$1,452
London	$399	$1,158
Sydney	$719	$1,408
Tel Aviv	$819	$1,650

Payment Methods: Cash, money order, certified check, personal check, Visa, MasterCard, American Express, wire transfer
In Business Since: 1987

Cut Throat can import tickets, and use "local currency strategies" to take advantage of market discrepancies. Because of fluctuations in the international monetary system, sometimes it is cheaper to buy a ticket in your destination country's local market (and local currency) than to buy the translated price in your home currency. Owner Mel Cohen says he will do the shopping for you, calling around to several wholesale consolidators to find you the best deal.

IBC Pacific (International Bonded Courier)

1595 El Segundo Boulevard
El Segundo, CA 90245 USA
☎ (310) 665 1760
Fax 310/ 665 0247

Times to Call: 9am to 4pm, Tuesday through Friday
Type of Provider: Courier company
Areas of Specialty: Pacific Rim

DESTINATIONS	SAMPLE ROUND-TRIP FARE	FULL COACH FARE	LENGTH OF STAY
Bangkok	$495	$1,452	7 to 18 days

Deposit: $500!
Payment Methods: Cash, money order, personal check, Visa, MasterCard
Courier Duties on Return Trip: Yes
Minimum Age: 21 years
In Business Since: 1988
Recommended Advance Reservations: 6 to 8 weeks
Luggage: Carry-on only

IBC books its San Francisco courier flights through agents at its Los Angeles office. The courier gets a paid hotel room in Tokyo for one night on the return leg of the flight.

Jupiter Air

839 Hinckley Road, Suite A
Burlingame, CA 94010 USA
☎ (415) 697 1773
Fax 415/ 697 7892
Contact: Ask for the calendar agent

Times to Call: 9am to 5pm

Type of Provider: Courier company

Areas of Specialty: Worldwide

DESTINATIONS	SAMPLE ROUND-TRIP FARE	FULL COACH FARE	LENGTH OF STAY
Bangkok	$370	$1,452	14 days
London	$350	$1,158	14 days
Manila	$455	$1,420	7 to 30 days
Singapore	$435	$1,080	7 to 30 days

Annual Fee: $35 for 3 years

Deposit: $100

Payment Methods: Cash, money order, certified check, personal check

Courier Duties on Return Trip: Yes

Minimum Age: 18 years

In Business Since: 1988

Recommended Advance Reservations: 0 to 3 months

Ask about last-minute discounts (50 percent off) and the cancellation phone list. London and Bangkok flights allow 2 checked bags.

Hong Kong is Jupiter Air's hub city. Thus it is sometimes possible to reserve a courier flight from Hong Kong to other Asian cities, such as Bangkok or Tokyo. Keep in mind that you must be back in Hong Kong in time for your return flight to San Francisco.

Additional offices in Hong Kong, London, Los Angeles, New York, Seoul, Sydney, Taipei, Tokyo. Jupiter strongly favors repeat business. Last-minute flights can be had for 50 percent off.

Omega World Travel

441 California Street

San Francisco, CA 94104 USA

☎ (800) 888 7372, (415) 956 0680

Fax 415/ 956 6227

Times to Call: 8:30am to 5:30pm

Type of Provider: Discount travel agent

Areas of Specialty: Europe, Middle East, domestic USA

Payment Methods: For TWA deal, accepts credit cards only.

In Business Since: 1970

By knowing to ask for the "TWA Global Discount fares," you will automatically get 20 percent off all domestic TWA fares, and 25 percent off all international fares. You get the same seat on the same flight—you just pay less. Call TWA first at ☎ (800) 221 2000 to get the flight number and lowest published fare for the flight you want, then call Omega World Travel to book the ticket. Senior and student fares are excluded from this offer. How do they do it? Under its restructuring plan, TWA owes investor Carl Icahn roughly $600 million. Carl has the right to buy TWA tickets at 40 percent or more off of published fares. He marks them up a bit and resells them, with the profit going to reduce TWA's debt. Omega buys from Carl's agent, and passes the 20 to 25 percent discount on to you. This deal will continue until the debt is paid in full, which will probably be in 1998 or later.

We list additional Omega offices in the Los Angeles, New York, and San Francisco chapters. Not near one of these cities? No problem. Omega has 280 offices nationwide. Call ☎ (800) 955 2582 to find the office nearest you.

STA Travel

51 Grant Avenue
San Francisco, CA 94108 USA
☎ (800) 2COUNCIL, (415) 391 8407
Fax 415/ 391 4105
Internet: http://www.sta-travel.com/

Times to Call: 9am to 5pm
Type of Provider: Discount travel agency
Areas of Specialty: Worldwide

DESTINATIONS	SAMPLE ROUND-TRIP FARE	FULL COACH FARE
Amsterdam	$630	$1,468
Bangkok	$749	$1,452
Frankfurt	$735	$1,558
Hong Kong	$563	$935
London	$515	$1,158
Singapore	$643	$1,080
Sydney	$914	$1,408
Tokyo	$615	$930

Payment Methods: Cash, money order, personal check, Visa, MasterCard

In Business Since: 1975

STA is the world's largest travel organization for students and young, independent travelers. They have 120 locations worldwide. Some of their best fares require student ID, or carry a maximum age.

Their tickets are highly flexible, usually good for one year, and require no advance purchase. Date changes can be made at any office world-wide for $25; refunds cost only $75. Such flexible tickets are a wise choice for travelers going on long trips without fully concrete itiner-aries. STA tickets are priced based on one-way tickets, which makes it easy to book open-jaw flights.

SunTrips

The SunTrips Building
2350 Paragon Drive
San Jose, CA 95131 USA
☎ (800) 786 8747, (408) 432 1101
Internet: http://www.suntrip.com/
Times to Call: 7:30am to 6:30pm weekdays, 9am to 4pm Saturday, 10am to 2pm Sunday
Type of Provider: Charter operator
Areas of Specialty: Europe, Mexico and domestic USA

DESTINATIONS	SAMPLE ROUND-TRIP FARE	FULL COACH FARE
Boston	$218	$840
Cancun	$229	$719
Honolulu	$219	$580
London	$398	$1,158
Mexico City	$189	$475
New York	$218	$862

Payment Methods: Cash, money order, personal check, Visa, MasterCard, American Express

In Business Since: 1976

SunTrips' coast-to-coast and London flights operate in spring and summer only.

Hawaii and coast-to-coast flights are scheduled service. Mexico and London are charter flights. London flights use Stansted Airport, which has a direct rail link to the London Underground's Liverpool Station. Most aircraft are provided and operated by Leisure Air, a major charter company.

Sundance / Travel Time

660 Market Street
San Francisco, CA 94105 USA
☎ (800) 322 8330, (415) 677 0799, (415) 398 8300
Fax 415/ 391 1856

Times to Call: 7:30am to 6pm
Type of Provider: Discount travel agency
Areas of Specialty: Mexico, Hawaii, Asia and Europe, including around- the-world

DESTINATIONS	SAMPLE ROUND-TRIP FARE	FULL COACH FARE
Amsterdam	$621	$1,468
Cancun	$269	$719
Honolulu	$219	$580
London	$600	$1,158
Maui	$239	$638
Mexico City	$219	$475

Payment Methods: Cash, personal check, Visa, MasterCard, American Express
In Business Since: 1983

Travel Time agents are specialists in particular regions, and are actually paid to visit their areas of expertise each year.

They also specialize in around-the-world, circle-Pacific, and other customized multi-stop itineraries. They can issue tickets originating and terminating anywhere in the world. Fax or e-mail (ehasbrouck @igc.apc.org) to save telephone charges from outside the USA.

UTL Travel

320 Corey Way

South San Francisco, CA 94080 USA

☎ (650) 583 5074

Fax 650/ 583 8122

Contact: Rosella

Times to Call: 9am to 6pm

Type of Provider: Courier booking agent

Areas of Specialty: Worldwide

DESTINATIONS	SAMPLE ROUND-TRIP FARE	FULL COACH FARE	LENGTH OF STAY
Bangkok	$405	$1,452	up to 30 days
London	$350	$1,158	14 days
Manila	$450	$1,420	up to 30 days
Singapore	$455	$1,080	up to 30 days

Deposit: $100

Payment Methods: Cash, money order, certified check

In Business Since: 1988

Recommended Advance Reservations: 2 to 3 months

Luggage: Varies by destination

Prices increase by $50 in June, July, August and December. UTL offers both last-minute discounts and a cancellation phone list. They are the booking agents for TNT Skypak and Jupiter Air.

AMSTERDAM, THE NETHERLANDS

MARKET TRENDS

Amsterdam is well-known for its consolidators. The famously permissive government lets agencies sell tickets for well below IATA fares. Amsterdam is particularly good for intra-European travel. For flights to other continents, the cheapest flights are still in London. Citizens of most of Asia, Africa, Eastern Europe, and Latin America need both visas and onward tickets in order to enter the country.

CHAPTER 8

STOPPING OVER IN AMSTERDAM

Amsterdam has maintained a penchant for the exotic ever since 17th-century Dutch explorers returned with such interesting novelties as tobacco, porcelain, coffee and rare spices. The spicy Indonesian rijsttafel ("rice table") was one of these wonderful imports, and is now a culinary must for those visiting the Netherlands.

As you might expect, canals and the harbor play a big part in the feel of this city, much of which is built below sea level. Tranquil strolls along the canals are in order, as is the panoramic harbor view seen on the ferry ride from Centraal Station to Amsterdam Noord.

Whether out of political expedience or respect for individual liberties, the Netherlands has some of the most permissive vice laws in the western world. Both soft drug use and prostitution are tolerated by the authorities. While you won't see large marijuana leaves painted on the doors of the cafés anymore (they've been replaced by green ferns in the window), the substance is still for sale inside. Absolutely avoid transporting any such substance outside of the country—foreign customs agents use dogs on the trains and buses leaving the Netherlands. The red-light district is another anomaly in western society. Lingerie-clad prostitutes pose in the windows of houses along canal-lined streets, as locals, tourists, and even couples stroll past. The area is said to be safe, probably due to the presence of voyeuristic crowds who seem driven to see this for themselves. Ironically, the district surrounds Oude Kerk, the city's oldest Gothic church.

Summertime is a great time to check out **Vondelpark**. The Dutch answer to New York's Central Park, the park was one giant camp-

TELEPHONE COUNTRY CODE:
(31)

CURRENCY:
Guilder
US$1 = f1.70
f1 = $0.59

ground for flower children in the Sixties. Nowadays, the campers have been replaced by street artists, who give way to regular concerts and plays in the open-air theater all summer long. If you are looking for quiet, escape into the wooded glens and lakes surrounding the theater. Visitors may want to stop for tea at the avant-garde **Ronde Blauwe Theehuis**, or relax at the terrace café of the nearby **Filmmuseum**.

A wide variety of nightlife options, from quiet chess cafés to rowdy punk performances, keeps the local scene interesting. Popular among both travelers and locals is the **Melkweg**, or Milky Way. This unique venue hosts art events, films, theater, poetry readings and (especially on weekends) live bands.

CHEAP SLEEPS

Bob's Youth Hostel

NZ Voorburgwal 92

☎ (020) 623 0063

An Amsterdam institution, Bob's downstairs café has been the meeting point for tens of thousands of backpack-toting explorers. A fun place to socialize, the café is also a good place for a cheap meal. Upstairs, clean, single-sex dorms run f20 a night. 3am curfew.

Sleepin Arena

's-Gravesandestraat 51-53

☎ (020) 694 7444

When everything else in town is full for the night, you can turn to this mega-hostel for help. Bunks in 100-person rooms go for f14, breakfast is f5 extra. Live bands and flower children are seen here frequently. No curfew. Metro: Weesperplein.

Hotel van Onna

Bloemgracht 102

☎ (020) 626 5801

Moving up a notch in price, the clean rooms go for f60 a person, in singles through quads. The pleasant, older Jordaan neighborhood has more cafés than tourists. Enjoy your breakfast and your view of the

canal, and venture out with the hordes only when you are good and
ready. Reservations recommended. Tram: No. 13 or 17 from Centraal
Station.

CHEAP EATS

Stalls at the Waterlooplein flea market purvey some of the cheapest
eats in the city. However, **Anno Vleminckx Sausmeesters**
(Voetboogstraat 33) gives the stalls stiff competition, serving up overflowing paper cones of French fries with sauce for f2. Pancakes are a
traditional Dutch supper item, and can be picked up at any of several dozen shops for under f10.

For great rijsttafel on a budget, head over to the Leidseplein. **Bojo**, at
Lange Leidsedwarstraat 51, has various Indonesian specialties, including rijsttafel, for about f16 a person. Open until 2am weeknights,
until 5am on Friday and Saturday.

TO & FROM THE AIRPORT

Netherlands Railways operates frequent, 24-hour service from the
basement of Amsterdam Schiphol Airport to the Centraal Station (16
minutes) for f4. You must purchase your ticket before boarding. For
those seeking convenience over savings, the KLM Shuttle bus departs
twice hourly from Schiphol, stopping at each of the major downtown
hotels. The fare is f20, payable to the driver, and the ride lasts 20 to
50 minutes.

UNIQUELY AMSTERDAM

Amsterdam is so bicycle-friendly that you can ride from Centraal
Station to the city's edge in half an hour. You will be amazed at how
abruptly the city ends and the farmhouses and countryside begin. The
surrounding area's many lakes and ponds lend it the name
Waterland. To get there, take your rented bicycle back behind the station to catch the free ferry across the IJ. Then follow Buiksloterweg,
turn right at Café Trefpunt, and follow the signs towards
Nieuwendam. You can follow the coastline to Uitdam (6 km from
Amsterdam), and then turn inland towards the village Broek in
Waterland (6km further). Those inspired by the ride can continue
another hour north to **Edam** (home of the cheese), while those who

have already satisfied their cycling urges can stop for the traditional post-ride pancake at **De Witte Swaen**. The Broek trip takes about three hours, while the Edam trip requires about five.

European Travel Network
Damrak 30

Amsterdam, NETHERLANDS

☎ (020) 622 6473

Fax 020/ 638 2271

Times to Call: 9am to 5pm

Type of Provider: Consolidator

Areas of Specialty: Asia, Africa, Latin America, Australia, North America

DESTINATIONS	SAMPLE ROUND-TRIP FARE	FULL COACH FARE
Delhi	f1,099	f2,440
Nairobi	f1,138	f5,882
Rio de Janeiro	f1,425	f4,226
Singapore	f1,245	f3,229
Sydney	f2,045	f3,836

Payment Methods: Cash, money order, certified check, personal check

In Business Since: 1974

They book flights for everywhere in the world except Europe.

Future Line Travel
Prof. Tulpplein 4

Amsterdam, NETHERLANDS

☎ (020) 622 2859

Fax 020/ 639 0199

Times to Call: 9am to 5pm

Type of Provider: Consolidator

Areas of Specialty: Worldwide

DESTINATIONS	SAMPLE ROUND-TRIP FARE	FULL COACH FARE
Bangkok	f1,290	f2,819

London	f393	f520	*From*
Los Angeles	f1,247	f2,550	*Amsterdam*
New York	f690	f1,945	
Sydney	f2,273	f3,836	
Tel Aviv	f999	f2,347	

Payment Methods: Cash, Visa, American Express, Eurocard
In Business Since: 1986

Future Line can ship tickets to buyers in other countries for a surcharge of f25. Youth hostel members receive a discount on the ferries to England. Also, Future Line can book youth hostels via their computer system.

NBBS Reizen

Haarlemmerstraat 115
1013EM Amsterdam NETHERLANDS
☎ (020) 626 2557
Fax 071/ 522 7243
Internet: http://www.sta-travel.com/

Times to Call: 9:30am to 5:30pm
Type of Provider: Discount travel agency
Areas of Specialty: Worldwide

DESTINATIONS	SAMPLE ROUND-TRIP FARE	FULL COACH FARE
Athens	f595	f3,265
Bangkok	f1,170	f2,819
Jakarta	f1,430	f2,300
London	f280	f520
Los Angeles	f1,195	f2,550
New York	f592	f1,945
Rome	f445	f2,392
Sydney	f1,980	f3,836

Payment Methods: Cash, bank transfer
In Business Since: 1975

Member of the STA Travel Network. STA is the world's largest travel organization for students and young, independent travelers. They have 120 locations worldwide. Some of their best fares require student ID or carry a maximum age.

107

Their tickets are highly flexible, usually good for one year and requiring no advance purchase. Date changes can be made at any office worldwide for $25; refunds cost only $75. Such flexible tickets are a wise choice for travelers going on long trips without fully concrete itineraries. STA tickets are priced based on one-way tickets, which makes it easy to book open-jaw flights.

Sister company Budget Air [☎ (020) 627 1251] does accept credit cards for the purchase of discount air travel, but cannot make changes on STA tickets.

Nouvelles Frontières

1 Van Baerlestraat #3

1071 A1 Amsterdam NETHERLANDS

☎ (020) 664 0447

Fax 020/ 675 3457

Internet: http://www.sv.vtcom.fr/nf/ (note: French language site)

Times to Call: 9am to 5pm

Type of Provider: Consolidator and charter operator

Areas of Specialty: Worldwide

DESTINATIONS	SAMPLE ROUND-TRIP FARE	FULL COACH FARE
Bangkok	f1,250	f2,819
Dakar	f1,200	f4,600
Delhi	f1,095	f2,440
London	f220	f520
Paris	f300	f1,039

Payment Methods: Cash, money order, certified check, personal check, Visa, MasterCard, American Express

In Business Since: 1967

Discount tickets on Tower Air, American Trans Air, Continental, KLM, American Airlines, and CORSAIR.

Started in 1967 by a French law student who was putting together a trip to Morocco for some friends. The entire trip cost a quarter of the price of a round-trip air ticket from Paris to Casablanca. Later, he organized a second trip for 300 people, and Nouvelles Frontières was born. They now have 132 offices worldwide, and some of the cheapest flights to or from the French-speaking world.

From
Amsterdam

Nouvelles Frontières fought the airline cartel in a landmark 1985 case before the European Court of Justice, and won the right to sell discounted airfares.

FRANKFURT, GERMANY

CHAPTER 9

MARKET TRENDS

Frankfurt Flughafen is the busiest airport in Germany, and the second busiest in Europe. The discount-ticket market is quite competitive, in spite of the government's disdain for consolidator-style discounts. But entrepreneurial spirit dies hard, and the German travel marketplace is no exception. While consolidators as such are well hidden, the market is overflowing with charter offerings. Tour operators (listed in this chapter as discount travel agents) and their charter flights offer your best chance for a budget flight out of Germany. Peruse the ads in the Friday or Saturday *Frankfurter Rundschau* to find additional budget flights. If flying courier strikes your fancy, Frankfurt's bankers produce mounds of documents that need to be somewhere else, fast. Generally speaking, low season is January to March, mid-season is April to August, and high season is September to December.

STOPPING OVER IN FRANKFURT

Once the home office of Hessian mercenary soldiers, Frankfurt is now the financial hub of Germany. Locals refer to it derisively as "Bankfurt," which may not be unfair. But Frankfurt is also the hub of German techno music and host of a major university, so you will run into black-clad poets just as often as briefcase-clutching number crunchers.

Even the formidable Hessians could not stop the Allies' relentless bombing during World War II. Virtually all of the city's historical buildings were flattened then, and have since been replaced with the skyscrapers of today's metropolis. Of course there are also less imposing neighborhoods, such as the relaxed and classic **Sachsen-hausen**, or the blue-collar and alternative **Bockenheim**, which is home to the university and an ethnically diverse population.

For nightlife reminiscent of New Orleans, check out **Jazzgasse** ("Jazz Alley"), officially known as Kleine Bockenheimer Strasse. Most nights you will find live music here, courtesy of some of Germany's finest jazz players.

If after a few days here you feel the urge to flee, consider getting a shared ride in a private car. A lot safer than hitchhiking, the

TELEPHONE
COUNTRY CODE:

(49)

CURRENCY:
Deutschemark
US$1 = 1.52DM
1DM = $0.66

Mitfahrzentrale office [near the Hauptbahnhof at Baseler Str. 7, ☎ (069) 23 64 44] matches riders with cars headed in the right direction. The drivers are usually students, to whom riders pay a token sum per kilometer of the ride.

CHEAP SLEEPS

Haus der Jugend (HI)
Deutschherrnufer 12
Frankfurt, GERMANY
☎ (069) 61 90 58

The best deal in Frankfurt, the Haus is located just a few blocks east of the museums and taverns in Sachsenhausen. Rates in dorm rooms start at 24DM, including linen and breakfast. Quads, doubles and singles run progressively higher. The midnight curfew is purely hypothetical, although you can pay a key deposit if you are worried about getting locked out. The pleasant patio space is great for meeting fellow travelers.

You are less likely to run into tourists and GIs in the Westend. Near the university and the Palmgarten, try **Pension Backer** at Mendelssohnstr. 92 [☎ (069) 74 79 92 or 74 79 00]. The location is more than respectable, and convenient to the Westend U-Bahn station. Singles go for 25-45DM, doubles for 65DM, triples for 85DM.

Camping is another option. Just west of Sachsenhausen you will find a site at Campingplatz Niederrader [Ufer 20, ☎ (069) 67 38 46]. Take Tram No. 15 from central Sachsenhausen.

CHEAP EATS

For apple wine and food like mom would make (if she were traditional and German), check out **Wagner**, at Schweitzer Str. 17 in Sachsenhausen. The atmosphere is lively and popular enough that you may have to wait for a table. Nearby **Nachteule** (Schifferstr. 3) is a well-known late-night hangout, with heaping plates pouring out of the kitchen until 4am.

In Bockenheim, when sausage and potatoes are getting you down, try **Ban Thai**. At Leipziger Str. 26, you'll get a nice contrast to the blandness of cabbage, for a decent price to boot.

If budgetary concerns pervade your consciousness, grab a hearty lunch at the **University Mensa**. This is a student cafeteria, so you'll need some remotely believable form of student ID to get the big discounts, like full meals for 4-6DM. No ID? You might never even be asked for it, and the regular prices are still reasonable. Located at Bockenheimer Landstr. 120, adjacent to U-Bahn Bockenheimer Warte. Open weekdays from 9am to 4pm.

TO & FROM THE AIRPORT

The national train company, Deutsche Bundesbahn (DB), operates a train from the airport's Bahnhof to the Hauptbahnhof. Trains depart every 15 minutes, and the trip lasts about 11 minutes. The fare is 5DM, from the ticket machine at the baggage claim in Terminal 1, Hall B (purchase ticket before boarding or face a 60DM fine). The city's FVV also runs two S-Bahn subway lines that connect the airport to the Hauptbahnhof. Interrail and Eurail tickets are valid on both the DB and the S-Bahn trains. From the Hauptbahnhof, you can catch a train to about anywhere in Europe, or catch tram #11 (or walk 15 minutes) to the old city center.

UNIQUELY FRANKFURT

A relaxing alternative to the claustrophobic metropolis is the mostly pedestrianized **Sachsenhausen** district, on the southern bank of the Main River. The "Pedestrians Only" restriction is probably a wise one, since this neighborhood is known as the "apple wine quarter," after the local and wildly popular specialty. The district is also home to the **Museumsufer**, a cluster of seven museums lined up on Schaumainkai. Wander through it as if at a food court, stopping here and there to sample the offerings. Many museums have free admission. On Saturdays, the Museumsufer hosts a large flea market (Flohmarkt), with stalls and museums combining in a wonderful "art and artifacts" motif.

Council Travel

Graf Adolf Strasse 64
40212 Dusseldorf GERMANY
☎ (0211) 36 30 30
Fax 0211/ 32 74 69
Internet: http://www.ciee.org/cts/ctshome.htm

Times to Call: 9am to 5pm
Type of Provider: Discount travel agent
Areas of Specialty: Worldwide

DESTINATIONS	SAMPLE ROUND-TRIP FARE	FULL COACH FARE
Bangkok	1,190DM	5,988DM
London	285DM	840DM
Los Angeles	690DM	6,300DM
New York	499DM	3,792DM

Payment Methods: Cash, personal check, electronic funds transfer
In Business Since: 1947

This office is not actually located in Frankfurt, but books many of its cheapest flights through there, and is reliably cheap enough to merit inclusion. Its best deals are on flights to the USA. One-way tickets available. Additional office in Munich [☎ (089) 39 50 22, fax 089/ 39 70 04].

(See the Council Travel listing on page 29 in the Chicago chapter for company background.)

Last Minute Borse

Bornheiner Landstrasse 60
Frankfurt/Main GERMANY
☎ (069) 44 00 01 or 44 00 02
Fax 069/ 493 0969

Times to Call: 9am to 5pm
(Lengthy informational recording in German available after hours.)
Type of Provider: Discount travel agent
Areas of Specialty: Worldwide

DESTINATIONS	SAMPLE ROUND-TRIP FARE	FULL COACH FARE
Athens	590DM	2,396DM
Bangkok	1,239DM	5,988DM
Jakarta	1,489DM	7,257DM
London	285DM	840DM
Los Angeles	999DM	6,300DM
Madrid	569DM	1,833DM
New York	529DM	3,792DM
Sydney	1,769DM	7,703DM
Tokyo	1,929DM	8,092DM

Payment Methods: Cash, money order, certified check, personal check, Visa, MasterCard, American Express

In Business Since: 1987

Linehaul Express

Flughafen Franchtzentrum, Geb. 453

60549 Frankfurt/Main GERMANY

☎ (069) 79 32 60

Fax 069/ 79 32 62

Contact: Claus Stelling

Times to Call: 9am to 5pm

Type of Provider: Courier company

Areas of Specialty: Asia and Australia

DESTINATIONS	SAMPLE ROUND-TRIP FARE	FULL COACH FARE	LENGTH OF STAY
Bangkok	1,100DM	5,988DM	up to 3 mos
Hong Kong	800DM	7,398DM	up to 3 mos
Manila	950DM	6,944DM	up to 3 mos
Osaka	1,250DM	8,080DM	up to 3 mos
Shanghai	1,150DM	7,572DM	up to 3 mos
Singapore	1,050DM	7,414DM	up to 3 mos
Taipei	975DM	7,119DM	up to 3 mos
Tokyo	1,250DM	8,092DM	up to 3 mos

Payment Methods: Cash, certified check, personal check, bank transfer

Courier Duties on Return Trip: Yes

Minimum Age: 18 years

A 50 percent down payment is required at the time of booking, with the remainder due 30 days before departure.

All flights require a stop in Hong Kong. A stay in Hong Kong is permitted, but not required. One-way flights are available on some sectors.

Because Linehaul Express is the general sales agent for Cathay Pacific Wholesale Courier, all flights are on Cathay Pacific Airlines. Linehaul can book excursion tickets in conjunction with their long-haul flights to many destinations in the Far East to which courier flights are not available. Additional Linehaul Express offices in London and Hong Kong.

STA Travel

Berger Strasse 118

60316 Frankfurt/Main GERMANY

☎ (069) 43 01 91

Fax 069/ 43 98 58

Internet: http://www.sta-travel.com/

Times to Call: 10am to 6pm

Type of Provider: Discount travel agency

Areas of Specialty: Worldwide

DESTINATIONS	SAMPLE ROUND-TRIP FARE	FULL COACH FARE
Athens	610DM	2,396DM
Bangkok	1,239DM	5,988DM
Jakarta	1,489DM	7,257DM
London	285DM	840DM
Los Angeles	999DM	6,300DM
Madrid	569DM	1,833DM
New York	529DM	3,792DM
Sydney	1,769DM	7,703DM
Tokyo	1,929DM	8,092DM

Payment Methods: Cash, bank transfer

In Business Since: 1975

Member of the STA Travel Network. STA is the world's largest travel organization for students and young, independent travelers. They have 120 locations worldwide. Some of their best fares require student ID, or carry a maximum age.

Their tickets are highly flexible, usually good for one year, and require no advance purchase. Date changes can be made at any office worldwide for $25; refunds cost only $75. Such flexible tickets are a wise choice for travelers going on long trips without fully concrete itineraries. STA tickets are priced based on one-way tickets, which makes it easy to book open-jaw flights.

LONDON, ENGLAND

MARKET TRENDS

The Mecca of budget travelers worldwide, London has it all. Penny-pinching pilgrims will find more charter flights and courier runs here than anywhere in the world. What's more, London is the birthplace of the bucket shop, a form of business which first showed up here a quarter of a century ago. You will find cheap flights to everywhere in the world, including such pricey destinations as Africa and South America. Check the weeklies (see Uniquely London, below) for the latest discount travel advertisements, or pick up a copy of the *Evening Standard*. As in San Francisco, some London bucket shops can sell tickets by mail to travelers outside Britain for travel between cities just about anywhere in the world.

Citizens of most of Asia, Africa, Eastern Europe, and Latin America need both visas and onward tickets in order to enter the country.

STOPPING OVER IN LONDON

London is immense, but it sprawls with a certain staid dignity that escapes the average metropolis. The classic architecture and scenic Thames make it a sight to see, while its varied, never-ending activity makes it enjoyable to visit.

Big Ben, red double-decker buses, and the ubiquitous fish-and-chip stands satisfy most preconceptions of London. But underlying all that is an infinite web of interesting subcultures and lively activity which would take more than one lifetime to explore thoroughly. Inside the ancient Roman walls of the one-square-mile **City of London** lies the banking hub of modern Europe. Just outside the walls is the **East End**, a down-and-dirty neighborhood now known as much for its artist colonies as for its role as home to Jack the Ripper. During the **Notting Hill Carnival** (early August), you will see more samba lines than sipping of tea, as the local West Indian community gives Rio de Janeiro some real competition.

Admit from the outstart that you simply cannot see it all, then make some educated decisions about where to spend your time. First-time visitors can orient themselves by taking a quick bus tour of London's

TELEPHONE COUNTRY CODE:
(44)

CURRENCY:
Pound
US$1 = £0.66
£1 = $1.51

famous sights and districts. **The Original London Transport Sightseeing Tour** whisks you through most of London in an open-top double-decker bus. The trip lasts 90 minutes. The £12 price is a better deal if you buy it after noon, because you can then use it to hop on and off the circuit all day on both the day of purchase and the next. Wait for a live guide (as opposed to a recording), found on every other bus.

Don't miss the boat trip down the **River Thames**. Ferries run every 20 minutes from Westminster Bridge to the Tower of London. The trip lasts 30 minutes, costs £3, and is a pleasant place to have a picnic lunch. Even better, continue under Tower Bridge all the way out to **Greenwich**, taking in some of the most spectacular views in London. Return to central London on the nifty trains of the Docklands Light Railway.

The **London Underground**, alias "the tube," makes it easy to move among the various neighborhoods of London. If you are staying for more than 3 days, get a weekly pass. Avoid the expensive London Visitor Travel Card, which at £33 no Londoner would dream of buying. Instead, get a one-week Zone 1 Travelcard for £12. On the rare occasion that you need to venture outside Zone 1, you pay a small add-on fare. You'll need a passport-style photo, which, when transformed into a London Transport ID card, makes for a good souvenir.

At **Hyde Park Speakers' Corner** on Sundays (tube: Marble Arch) you can listen to some very polished political satirists, although you will have to find them amidst the religious zealots and the crazies. If you find yourself so inspired, you can speak, too.

Nobody knows exactly how many museums there are in London, but two not to be missed are the **Tate Gallery** (for Impressionist and Modernist works), and the **Museum of London** (the key to understanding London from prehistoric times to today).

Pubs, short for public houses, are neighborhood places where people go to talk (and drink). The farther you go from the touristy neighborhoods, the more likely you can strike up a conversation with the locals. If people start buying rounds, get your turn in early, before the group gets too big.

London has as broad and diverse a theater scene as New York, and

the tickets here are cheaper. In fact, high-altitude student seats for
the **Royal Shakespeare Company** can be bought from their box
office for just £1! Of course, you will have to sneak down into better
seats at intermission. Other theatrical offerings, ranging from musi-
cals to sex comedies, also offer student and standing-room discounts.
The afternoon of the show, tickets for some performances are on sale
at the half-price booth on Leicester Square. Other forms of nightlife
can be a bit pricey in London. One good choice for live bands and
modern rock is **The Borderline** (on Trafalgar Square) where the cover
rarely exceeds £5.

Of course, a visit to London only is a ridiculously one-sided way to see
Britain. For glorious contrast, try to arrange a brief escape to the
countryside. One delightful choice is the mountainous **Lake District.**
Hike through the fells, picnicking your way from village to village. A
bus to **Keswick** is all you really need; from there, friendly locals make
hitch-hiking easy (although, our lawyers point out, this is specifically
risky and not recommended). Energetic "peak baggers" can hike to
their hearts' content. Consider staying on a working sheep ranch!
Margaret Harryman and her family run a cozy, traditional English bed
and breakfast from their ranch house. Her young sons are quite
knowledgeable about sheep, and will gleefully take you on a tour of
the whole operation. Great breakfasts, and hostel-level prices
[**Keskadale Farm** Newlands Valley, Keswick, Cumbria CA12 5TS
England, ☎ (0171) 68 77 85 44]. Insider's Tip: go in lambing season,
which starts in March.

CHEAP SLEEPS

Oxford Street Youth Hostel (HI)
14-18 Noel Street
London W1 ENGLAND
☎ (0171) 734 1618

The happening, central location of this place means it fills up fast.
Either book way ahead of time by mail, or call a few days in advance
to try to reserve a spot. The famous Soho club scene surrounds you,
and, conveniently, there is no curfew here. Dorm beds in doubles
through quads run £18 for nonmembers, £15 for members. Tube:
Oxford Circus.

Dean Court Hotel

57 Inverness Terrace

London W2 ENGLAND

☎ (0171) 229 2961

Fax 0171/ 727 1190

More of a guest house than a hotel, this place is popular with the young "world traveler" set. Aussies and others take advantage of the weekly and monthly discounts to stay and work in London for a while. The neighborhood is working class, but very close to Kensington Gardens and Hyde Park, and to the Bayswater and Queensway tube stops. Dorm beds in a quad run £14, doubles are £35. The downstairs lounge is a good place to meet other travelers. Breakfast is included, and you can use the kitchen the rest of the day.

Woodville House

107 Ebury Street, Belgravia

London SW1W 9QU ENGLAND

☎ (0171) 730 1048

Fax 0171/ 730 2574

A classic bed and breakfast, Woodville has small, pleasantly appointed rooms and is conveniently located near Victoria Station. Hostess Rachel Joplin and her husband Ian are the reason this place is a real find. Rachel knows everything there is to know about London, and will help put you on the right track. Looking for a particular restaurant by name? Or is it that you need a little help in choosing that hopelessly romantic spot? Ask Rachel. She can even tell you how to get there by public transit. Ask, too, about Sue Ryder—the Harrods of charity shops. Singles are £36, doubles run about £56, and bunk rooms go for £18 to £25 per person. Nearby, you can lose yourself in the lush gardens surrounding Buckingham Palace.

CHEAP EATS

The meat stalls at **Old Spitalfields Market**, formerly a huge cattle emporium in the rough-edged East End, have been taken over by artists and crafts vendors. The center of the market houses a bizarre fairy tale-inspired sculpture installation, in which trains, musical fountains, and electric-powered humanoids perambulate every 15 minutes. Also in the center is a stage where post-avantgarde fashions are shown, and a pair of indoor athletic fields. Why all this in the Cheap Eats section? Because half a dozen exotic food stalls make their homes in the middle of all this, and you can eat lunch for a couple of pounds. A very genuine tapas restaurant has been plucked straight out of Madrid and dropped down here, too. Take the tube to Liverpool Street station, cross Bishopsgate, and continue two blocks northeast on Brushfield Street.

For a basic English meal, try the **Chelsea Kitchen** (98 Kings Road, SW3), or sister restaurant **The Stockpot** (50 James Street, W1). Both places live up to their motto, "Good meals at prices you can afford." Expect to eat well for under £5 per person. To spice things up a little, head over to the **Great India Restaurant**, at 79 Lower Sloane Street.

TO & FROM THE AIRPORT

From London Heathrow: Ah, direct service to the airport on the city subway system. Other cities (including San Francisco) could learn from London. The Tube's Picadilly Line runs every 5 to 10 minutes from Heathrow through the heart of the city (50 minutes). The fare is £3, and you can get to just about anywhere in London with no more than one transfer.

From London Gatwick: Catch British Rail's Gatwick Express, which runs every 15 minutes from the South Terminal to Victoria Station for £13, or £9 Second Class. By bus, catch the Flightline No. 777 from North or South Terminals to Victoria Coach Station (70 minutes), with hourly departures for £8.

From London Stansted: British Rail's Stansted Express runs twice hourly to London's Liverpool Street Station (30 minutes) for £10. By bus, catch the hourly National Express (No. 102, or 097, 098 or 099) to Victoria Coach Station (80 minutes) for £10.

UNIQUELY LONDON

Whatever your fancy, London probably has a club (or two) dedicated exclusively to bringing together people with a shared interest in doing it. The single best way to get off the beaten track in London is to find a group with which you share an interest, and get involved with them. Group meetings are usually free and open to the public. For fairly mainstream groups, as well as weekly concerts and such, pick up one of the London weeklies, such as *Time Out*, *TNT* and *What's On*. For intellectual pursuits, check out the bulletin boards in the buildings of the University of London's central campus (tube: Russell Square).

Feel like just hanging out? On weekends, British youth descend upon **Camden Market**, the hippest of the outdoor bazaars, to do exactly that. Just off the historic waterways of Camden Lock, near the Camden Town tube station, this is a great place to peruse used clothing, books and records. By day, grab a table at a café and watch the people, or cruise the stalls and strike up a conversation. By night, you'll find a lively bar scene, and clubs offering everything from jazz bands to the latest house music.

Afro-Asian Travel

162/168 Regent Street, Suite 233

London W1R 5TB ENGLAND

☎ (0171) 437 8255

Fax 0171/ 437 8250

Times to Call: 9:30am to 5:30pm

Type of Provider: Consolidator

Areas of Specialty: Africa, Asia, India

DESTINATIONS	SAMPLE ROUND-TRIP FARE	FULL COACH FARE
Bangkok	£330	£2,102
Bombay	£385	£1,024
Cairo	£265	£918
Johannesburg	£500	£1,122
Los Angeles	£340	£963
Nairobi	£440	£820
Sydney	£680	£1,266
Tel Aviv	£250	£723

Payment Methods: Cash, money order, certified check, personal check, Visa, MasterCard, Access, American Express

In Business Since: 1971

This company prides itself on its focus on personal service. There is a small surcharge for credit card purchases. The owner started out selling charter flights from London to Kenya, and gradually shifted into consolidated tickets.

Bridges Worldwide

Travel Dept., Old Mill House, Mill Road

West Drayton, Middlesex UB7 7EJ ENGLAND

☎ (0189) 546 5065

Fax 0189/ 546 5100

Contact: Stuart Martin or Elizabeth Guildera

Times to Call: 9am to 5:30pm

Type of Provider: Courier booking agent

Areas of Specialty: Worldwide

	DESTINATIONS	SAMPLE ROUND-TRIP FARE	FULL COACH FARE	LENGTH OF STAY
From	Bangkok	£325	£2,102	10 to 180 days
London	Larnaca	£500	£830	2 to 28 days
	Los Angeles	£275	£963	2 to 42 days
	New York	£200	£463	2 to 42 days
	San Francisco	£275	£963	2 to 42 days
	Tokyo	£500	£1,053	2 to 42 days

Payment Methods: Cash, certified check, personal check, Visa, MasterCard

Courier Duties on Return Trip: No

Minimum Age: 18 years

In Business Since: 1992

Recommended Advance Reservations: 3 months in high season

Luggage: Couriers are allowed to bring 23 kilograms of checked baggage, as well as their carry-ons

Bridges staff say "definitely" call to check on last-minute discounts. This company maintains a cancellation phone list. Some one-way tickets available for 60 percent of the round-trip fare, especially to Hong Kong.

Other originating cities include Bangkok, Hong Kong, and San Francisco. Bridges is the booking agent for courier flights on Virgin Express runs, so all flights are on Virgin Atlantic.

British Airways Travel Shops

World Cargo Centre, Export Cargo Terminal S126
Heathrow Airport, Hounslow TW6 2JS ENGLAND
☎ (0181) 564 7009
Fax 0181/ 562 6177

Times to Call: 9am to 5pm

Type of Provider: Courier booking agent

Areas of Specialty: Worldwide

DESTINATIONS	SAMPLE ROUND-TRIP FARE	FULL COACH FARE	LENGTH OF STAY
Bahrain	£250	£992	7 days
Bangkok	£348	£2,102	14 days
Barcelona	£80	£380	7 days
Boston	£180	£453	7 or 14 days

Budapest	£99	£616	7 days	*From*
Buenos Aires	£360	n/a	15 days	*London*
Cairo	£130	£918	7 days	
Chicago	£348	£942	7 or 14 days	
Dubai	£250	£1,110	7 days	
Gaborone	£350	£1,388	8 days	
Geneva	£99	£313	7 days	
Harare	£220	£2,012	10 or 11 days	
Hong Kong	£348	£1,166	7 days	
Johannesburg	£448	£1,122	14 or 21 days	
Kuala Lumpur	£348	£1,193	14 days	
Larnaca	£175	£830	7 or 8 days	
Lisbon	£80	£368	7 days	
Los Angeles	£250	£963	7 or 14 days	
Mauritius Isl.	£428	n/a	15 days	
Mexico City	£180	£956	14 days	
Miami	£150	£648	7 or 14 days	
Milan	£99	£398	7 days	
Montreal	£180	£680	7 days	
Nairobi	£260	£820	10 days	
New York	£180	£463	7 or 14 days	
Philadelphia	£180	£660	7 or 14 days	
Rio de Janeiro	£368	£1,598	15 days	
Rome	£99	£398	7 days	
San Francisco	£250	£963	7 or 14 days	
Seattle	£250	£963	7 or 14 days	
Singapore	£348	£889	14 days	
Stockholm	£99	£430	7 days	
Tel Aviv	£100	£723	7 days	
Tokyo	£498	£1,053	14 or days	
Toronto	£180	£680	7 or 14 days	
Washington DC	£180	£512	7 days	
Zurich	£99	£348	7 days	

Payment Methods: Cash, personal check, Visa, MasterCard

Courier Duties on Return Trip: No

Minimum Age: 18 years

In Business Since: 1992

Recommended Advance Reservations: 2 months

Luggage: On most flights, couriers are allowed to bring 23 kilograms of checked baggage, as well as one carry-on. No refunds for cancellations.

Campus Travel

52 Grosvenor Gardens

London SW1W OAG ENGLAND

☎ (0171) 730 3402

Internet: http://www.campustravel.co.uk

Times to Call: 9am to 6:30pm weekdays, plus Thursday open until 8pm, 10am to 6:30pm Saturday

Type of Provider: Discount travel agent

Areas of Specialty: Worldwide student and youth fares, including around-the-world

DESTINATIONS	SAMPLE ROUND-TRIP FARE	FULL COACH FARE
Amsterdam	£130	£195
Bangkok	£734	£2,102
Hong Kong	£900	£1,166
Los Angeles	£598	£963
Mexico City	£588	£956
New York	£330	£463
Paris	£134	£260
Prague	£258	£380
Sydney	£958	£1,266

Payment Methods: Cash, personal check, debit card, traveler's checks in sterling, Visa, MasterCard, American Express

In Business Since: 1959

This main office is located just across the street from Victoria Station. There are 36 other Campus Travel offices in the university towns across the UK, and about 500 affiliated offices worldwide. Campus Travel also books adventure tours and treks geared towards the student market.

Council Travel

28A Poland Street (off Oxford Circus)

London W1V 3DB ENGLAND

☎ (0171) 437 7767 for worldwide information

☎ (0171) 287 3337 for European information

Fax 0171/ 287 9414

Internet: http://www.ciee.org/cts/ctshome.htm

Times to Call: 9am to 6pm Monday to Saturday (9am to 7pm
Thursday), 10am to 5pm Sunday

Type of Provider: Discount travel agent

Areas of Specialty: Worldwide student, youth, and budget travel

DESTINATIONS	SAMPLE ROUND-TRIP FARE	FULL COACH FARE
Amsterdam	£68	£195
Bali	£505	£905
Bangkok	£345	£2,102
Los Angeles	£302	£963
New York	£233	£463
Paris	£68	£260
Prague	£129	£380
Sydney	£675	£1,266
Tel Aviv	£261	£723

Payment Methods: Cash, money order, personal check, Visa,
MasterCard, Access

In Business Since: 1947

Expect prices to drop a bit at the last minute, as specials come out a
few weeks before the date of departure.

(See the Council Travel listing on page 29 in the Chicago chapter for
company background.)

Courier Travel Services, Ltd.

346 Fulham Road

London, SW10 9UH ENGLAND

☎ (0171) 351 0300

Fax 0171/ 351 0170

Times to Call: 9am to 5:30pm

Type of Provider: Courier booking company

Areas of Specialty: Worldwide

DESTINATIONS	SAMPLE ROUND-TRIP FARE	FULL COACH FARE	LENGTH OF STAY
Cairo	£150	£918	up to 28 days
Harare	£435	£2,012	up to 28 days
Hong Kong	£449	£1,166	up to 28 days
Lusaka	£350	£1,600	7 or 15 days
Miami	£199	£648	up to 28 days
Nairobi	£399	£820	up to 28 days
New York	£179	£463	8 or 15 days
Port Louis	£499	n/a	15 days
Rio de Janeiro	£389	£1,598	up to 28 days
San Francisco	£265	£963	up to 28 days
Tokyo	£429	£1,053	up to 28 days

Payment Methods: Cash, money order, certified check, personal check, Visa, MasterCard, American Express
Courier Duties on Return Trip: Yes
Minimum Age: 18 years
In Business Since: 1989
Recommended Advance Reservations: 6 to 8 weeks
Luggage: 23 kilograms of checked luggage, plus carry-ons

One-way tickets available to Tokyo for £225. Call to check on last-minute discounts, which are extremely cheap. This company maintains a cancellation phone list. All flights are on British Airways. Couriers must complete a registration form before becoming eligible to book flights.

Going Abroad Travel Ltd.

417 Hendon Way
London NW4 3LH ENGLAND
☎ (0181) 202 0111
Fax 0181/ 202 3839

Times to Call: 9am to 5:30pm
Type of Provider: Consolidator
Areas of Specialty: Europe

DESTINATIONS	SAMPLE ROUND-TRIP FARE	FULL COACH FARE		*From*
Amsterdam	£75	£195		*London*
Athens	£99	£520		
Istanbul	£140	£572		
Paris	£69	£260		
Rome	£115	£398		
Tel Aviv	£149	£723		

Payment Methods: Cash, money order, personal check, debit card, Visa, MasterCard, American Express (a small fee is charged for use of American Express)

In Business Since: 1992

Those seeking to buy a ticket from abroad should inquire by fax, in order to save on telephone charges. They will respond by fax in a couple of hours.

Jupiter Air U.K., Ltd.

Jupiter House, Horton Road
Colnbrook, Slough SL3 0BB ENGLAND
☎ (0175) 368 9989
Fax 0175/ 368 1661
Contact: Peter Gill or Claire

Times to Call: 9am to 5pm
Type of Provider: Courier company
Areas of Specialty: Worldwide

DESTINATIONS	SAMPLE ROUND-TRIP FARE	FULL COACH FARE	LENGTH OF STAY
Hong Kong	tba	£1,106	tba
New York	£185	£463	1 or 4 weeks
Sydney	£550	£1,266	7 to 30 days

Payment Methods: Cash, personal check, Visa, MasterCard
In Business Since: 1988
Courier Duties on Return Trip: Yes
Recommended Advance Reservations: 0 to 3 months
Luggage: 20 kilograms of checked luggage plus carry-on

Hong Kong is Jupiter Air's hub city. Thus it is sometimes possible to reserve a courier flight from Hong Kong to other Asian cities, such as Bangkok or Tokyo. Keep in mind that you must be back in Hong Kong in time for your return flight.

This office is located near Heathrow Airport, west of London. Additional offices in Hong Kong, Los Angeles, New York, San Francisco, Seoul, Sydney, Taipei, and Tokyo. Jupiter strongly favors repeat business. One-way fares are available to all destinations. Last-minute flights can be had for 50 percent off. They also maintain a cancellation phone list.

Linehaul Express, Ltd.

Building 252, Section D
Ely Road, Heathrow Airport
Middlesex TW6 2PR ENGLAND
☎ (0181) 759 5969
Fax 0181/ 759 5973
Contact: Jill

Times to Call: 8:30am to 4:30pm
Type of Provider: Courier company
Areas of Specialty: Hong Kong and Australia

DESTINATIONS	SAMPLE ROUND-TRIP FARE	FULL COACH FARE	LENGTH OF STAY
Hong Kong	£350	£1,166	up to 3 mos
Sydney	£395	£1,266	up to 3 mos

Deposit: £100
Payment Methods: Cash, check, Visa
Courier Duties on Return Trip: Yes
Minimum Age: 18 years
In Business Since: 1989
Recommended Advance Reservations: 3 months

These flights are available as departures from either London or Manchester. One-way tickets to Hong Kong are available for a bit more than half the round-trip price. Flights to Sydney are round-trip only. This company maintains a cancellation phone list. Courier duties are performed on the outbound flight only.

Linehaul is the general sales agent for Cathay Pacific's courier operation, so all flights are on service-oriented Cathay Pacific Airlines. Additional Linehaul Express offices in Frankfurt and Hong Kong.

Nouvelles Frontières

11 Blenheim Street

London W1Y 9LE ENGLAND

☎ (0171) 355 3952 or 629 7772

Fax 0171/ 491 0684

Internet: http://www.sv.vtcom.fr/nf/ (note: French language site)

Times to Call: 9am to 5pm

Type of Provider: Consolidator and charter operator

Areas of Specialty: Worldwide

DESTINATIONS	SAMPLE ROUND-TRIP FARE	FULL COACH FARE
Agadir	£199	£638
Crete	£135	£598
Nice	£135	£294
Paris	£79	£260
Toulouse	£145	£294

Payment Methods: Cash, money order, certified check, personal check, Visa, MasterCard, American Express

In Business Since: 1967

Discount tickets on Tower Air, American Trans Air, Continental, KLM, American Airlines, and CORSAIR.

Started in 1967 by a French law student who was putting together a trip to Morocco for some friends. The entire trip cost a quarter of the price of a round-trip air ticket from Paris to Casablanca. Later, he organized a second trip for 300 people, and Nouvelles Frontières was born. They now have 132 offices worldwide, and some of the cheapest flights to or from the French-speaking world.

Nouvelles Frontières fought the airline cartel in a landmark 1985 case before the European Court of Justice, and won the right to sell discounted airfares.

STA Travel

117 Euston Road

London NW1 2SX ENGLAND

☎ (0171) 361 6161 for travel within Europe

☎ (0171) 361 6262 worldwide

Fax 0171/ 368 0075

Internet: http://www.sta-travel.com/

Times to Call: 8am to 7pm

Type of Provider: Discount travel agency

Areas of Specialty: Worldwide

DESTINATIONS	SAMPLE ROUND-TRIP FARE	FULL COACH FARE
Amsterdam	£69	£195
Bangkok	£357	£2,102
Ho Chi Minh City	£499	n/a
Los Angeles	£239	£963
Madrid	£84	£459
Mexico City	£286	£956
New York	£156	£463
Paris	£69	£260
Rio de Janeiro	£399	£1,598
Sydney	£622	£1,266

Payment Methods: Cash, money order, certified check, personal check, Visa, MasterCard, American Express

In Business Since: 1975

STA is the world's largest travel organization for students and young, independent travelers. They have 120 locations worldwide. Some of their best fares require student ID or carry a maximum age.

Their tickets are highly flexible, usually good for one year, and require no advance purchase. Date changes can be made at any office world-wide for $25; refunds cost only $75. Such flexible tickets are a wise choice for travelers going on long trips without fully concrete itiner-aries. STA tickets are priced based on one-way tickets, which makes it easy to book open-jaw flights.

Trailfinders

194 Kensington High Street

London W8 7RG ENGLAND

☎ (0171) 938 3232 for flights to Europe and transatlantic

☎ (0171) 938 3939 for flights elsewhere

Fax 0171/ 938 3305

Times to Call: 9am to 6pm Monday to Saturday (9am to 7pm Thursday), 10am to 4pm Sunday

Type of Provider: Consolidator

Areas of Specialty: Worldwide

DESTINATIONS	SAMPLE ROUND-TRIP FARE	FULL COACH FARE
Bangkok	£396	£2,102
Johannesburg	£415	£1,122
New York	£175	£463
Paris	£69	£260
Sydney	£469	£1,266
Tel Aviv	£239	£723

Payment Methods: Cash, money order, personal check, Visa, MasterCard, American Express

In Business Since: 1970

Trailfinders asks us to point out that they are unable to sell discounted fares for travel commencing outside the UK. In practice, this means that people starting from the Continent, for example, need to fly to London, and then start their discount itinerary from there. This is in fact a common occurrence, and can result in very substantial savings. These conditions are imposed by the airlines, and Trailfinders does enforce them strictly.

Trailfinders is one of the most well-known and well-respected consolidators in the world. They have added a "one-stop travel shop" which includes an immunization center, visa service, sales of American Express traveler's checks, book shop, bureau de change and a reference library. When paying by personal check, an eight-day hold is required before tickets can be issued.

USA Travel Centre, Ltd.

8 Hogarth Road
Earls Court
London SW5 0PT ENGLAND
☎ (0171) 373 8383, 835 1189
Fax 0171/ 373 3323

Times to Call: 9am to 5pm
Type of Provider: Charter operator
Areas of Specialty: USA

DESTINATIONS	SAMPLE ROUND-TRIP FARE	FULL COACH FARE
Athens	£139	£520
Los Angeles	£269	£963
Miami	£299	£648
New York	£199	£463
Orlando	£199	£648
Rome	£139	£398

Payment Methods: Cash, certified check, personal check, Visa, MasterCard, American Express
In Business Since: 1991

Works with tourist bureaus in each of the 50 states to promote British tourism in the USA. Also books a lot of flights for Americans traveling from London to the continent. The USA Travel Centre books flights on major carriers such as Virgin Atlantic, as well as charter companies such as American Trans Air.

Worldwide Cheap Travel Service

First Floor, 254 Earls Court Road
London SW5 9AD ENGLAND
☎ (0171) 373 6465
Fax 0171/ 370 3425

Times to Call: 10am to 6:30pm Monday to Friday, 10am to 5pm Saturday
Type of Provider: Consolidator
Areas of Specialty: Worldwide

DESTINATIONS	SAMPLE ROUND-TRIP FARE	FULL COACH FARE	*From*
Bangkok	£320	£2,102	*London*
Los Angeles	£299	£963	
Paris	£69	£260	
Sydney	£599	£1,266	
Tel Aviv	£169	£723	

Payment Methods: Cash, money order, certified check, personal
check, Visa, MasterCard, American Express

In Business Since: 1981

WCTS specializes in cheap flights to Europe and the Far East. They
can also get you deals on business and first-class flights to and from
the USA.

BANGKOK, THAILAND

CHAPTER 11

MARKET TRENDS

Thailand teems with budget airfare opportunities, but some caution is advised. Consolidators congregate near the guest houses on Khao San Road, and near the Malaysia Hotel. Convincing but fake student IDs can be purchased from sidewalk vendors in the same neighborhoods. Avoid J Travel (near the Malaysia Hotel) and Come & Go Travel (behind *Wat Chanasongkhram*, at the foot of Khao San Road)—people have complained about them for decades. Keep an ear to the street. You will hear the latest news about companies who sell tickets on planes that do not exist. Luckily, credit cards are widely accepted.

Many travelers consider Bangkok the gateway to Burma, Cambodia and Vietnam. This can be true, but for a quick trip, many U.S. and British consolidators can get you a better deal if you book straight through to your final destination (with an optional stopover in Bangkok, but all on one ticket). Local travel agents can usually arrange visas for you for a small fee.

Courier flights from Bangkok can be fantastic deals for those taking quick trips. On occasion, companies will sell (and even give away) one-way courier flights at the last minute, so it can be worthwhile to call and ask.

Thai customs officials will accept "sufficient funds" as proof that you can support yourself in the country. No onward ticket is required, just show them that you have enough cash in your moneybelt.

STOPPING OVER IN BANGKOK

Bangkok can seem overwhelming at first. Visitors are greeted by a cacophony of blaring motorscooter horns, roaring tuk tuks, singsonging vendors, and glittering temples, all shrouded at times by the faint, sweet scent of rotting vegetation or the acrid tang of car exhaust.

TELEPHONE COUNTRY CODE:

(66)

CURRENCY:
Baht
US$1 = 25B
1B = $.04

The sheer number of *wats*, or Buddhist temples, can also be overwhelming. There are almost 400 of these traditional sites in Bangkok alone. One of the most famous is **Wat Po**, home of the reclining Buddha, which is located along the Chaophrya River just south of the

Grand Palace and on the southern fringe of Banglampoo. It is also peaceful to wander through the beautifully landscaped grounds of some of the smaller neighborhood wats.

The **Grand Palace** and **Temple of the Emerald Buddha** are crowded with tourists, but still important to visit. Bear in mind the dress code: no leather shoes, no shorts and no sleeveless shirts. You can always rent appropriate apparel from vendors outside the site.

A note on prostitution. Admittedly, it happens in all parts of the world. What makes the Asian sex trade different is that some prostitutes are literally girls, usually 12 to 14 years old, sometimes younger. They are not consenting adults, and are not typically in this trade by choice. Most likely they have been drugged, kidnapped, or even sold by their own parents into the brothels. They will almost assuredly die of AIDS by age 25. Consider the implications carefully before you support this wretched business.

The feel you get for Bangkok can depend on the weather while you are there. In the really hot, dry times, people can seem worn out and are less likely to make the effort to be friendly. So a visit during dusty, hot and polluted April will be a lot different than a trip during cool and relaxing December. Rains are heaviest from June to November.

River sightseeing tip: take the public river taxis instead of hiring your own boat. When you share a "long-tailed taxi" *(rua hang yao)* with the locals, you get to experience dogs and babies coming out to the dock's end to greet whomever is coming home. The rua hang yao (10B) go up the same side canals for much less than the private boat tours (750B), and they are infinitely more social and entertaining. The private boat operators may tell you that the public taxis don't exist— don't believe a word of it. Stay by the pier and watch what happens. And pay the public taxi operator only what everyone else is paying— as a *farang* (foreigner), you can be seen as an easy mark. If the taxi stops for lunch somewhere, be flexible, and take the opportunity to do some off-the-beaten-track exploring.

If you must attempt to forge the gridlocked streets, there is rarely a need to splurge on a land-based taxi. The extensive bus network is crowded, but very cheap. Fares are under 5B. Before you leave home, stop at your local travel bookstore to pick up a copy of Bangkok's best map, by Nelles Verlag. If you wait until you get there, you'll have to make do with the *No. 1 Best Seller* map. The good thing about this yellow, green and red map is that it identifies all sites in both English and Thai script, making it easy for any passerby to locate your destination. It also shows bus routes. During the daytime traffic, your best urban land travel option may well be the plentiful motorcycle taxis. It is risky, and not much cheaper than a traditional taxi, but it is infinitely faster in traffic (just don't tell your mom!)

Bangkok can be crowded and oppressive, so if you can stay for more than a few days, consider taking the three-hour train ride from Thonburi Station to **Kanchanaburi**. This laid-back small city is very popular with Thai tourists, due largely to its scenic location, which was portrayed in the movie *Bridge over the River Kwai*. Stay in a riverside bungalow for 10B a night. **Rick's Lodge** is a good choice, since they have a great restaurant and speak perfect English.

CHEAP SLEEPS

Try to stay in places near the river, because travel by river is much more pleasant than travel in a steamy, gridlock-bound taxi. You'll find the three- and four-star hotels in the **Sukumvit** and **Siam** districts, but they are a bit far from the markets, temples, clubs and backpackers in the **Banglampoo** area. Khao San Road is the best-known street in Banglampoo, so the two terms are roughly synonymous. Keep in mind that taxi drivers get a commission for bringing guests to certain guest houses, so be insistent if they tell you that the place you wanted to go has burned down, closed for health reasons, etc.

The high season for tourism is January and February, during which time it is wise to reserve rooms in advance, or at least start looking early in the morning before the best places are taken.

Because so many travelers stay on Khao San Road, it has become somewhat of a backpackers' ghetto. By walking a mere ten minutes to the north you will find a quieter, more authentically Thai neighborhood which locals describe as "what Khao San Road was like ten years ago." The businesses here cater mostly to local families, whom you will see strolling along the streets. To get there, walk north along Samsen Road, and turn left at the National Library. Or from the airport, take air conditioned bus No. 10 to Samsen Road / the National Library.

Shanti Lodge

37 Sri Ayuthaya Road

Bangkok 10300 THAILAND

☎ (02) 281 2497

Shanti's peaceful open-air café area, centered around a trickling garden fountain, is blessedly different from Khao San Road's TV bars. Shared tables make it easy to meet other hip travelers. Dorm rooms run 70B, doubles run about 200B, and the "VIP Room," complete with air conditioning and its own television, goes for 400B. No singles, although you could spring for a double. The all-vegetarian food is excellent, and the staff is genuinely warm and welcoming.

Tavee Guest House

37 Sri Ayuthaya Road Soi 14

Bangkok 10300 THAILAND

☎ (02) 282 5983, or 280 1447

Almost next door to Shanti, Tavee has multiple common lounges and a garden restaurant. Fairly large rooms with fans run 120B for singles or 180B for doubles.

New Siam Guest House

21 Soi Chanasongkhram, Phra Athit

Bangkok 10200 THAILAND

☎ (02) 282 4554

Fax 02/ 281 7461

New Siam is behind the temple at the foot of Khao San Road, on an alley near the Phra Athit express river-taxi stop. Singles run 180B, doubles 260B, and doubles with bath 360B. Their best rooms, which go for about 450B a night, include air-conditioning, private bath with shower curtains and similar amenities that are rare for this price. Lockers, good breakfasts and a travel agency are all downstairs. Young crowd. Five floors of smallish rooms are packed with *farangs* from around the world, making this a place where the service is not personal, but there's always someone new to share travel stories with.

Prakorb's House

52 Khao San Road, Banglampoo

Bangkok 10200 THAILAND

☎ (02) 281 1345

Fax 02/ 629 0714

If you must stay on chaotic Khao San Road itself, Prakorb's is a good choice. Friendly and informative host Aswin Prakorb runs an efficient small café downstairs, and a fairly priced guest house upstairs. The small singles are reminiscent of early-seventies Eastern Block public housing, but at 90B, who's to complain? On the other hand, the doubles are spacious rooms in a traditional Thai-style teak building, which are a steal at 180B. All rooms have fans.

CHEAP EATS

There seems to be more food for sale in Bangkok than anywhere else in the world. It is as if the Thais never eat at home. You will find lots of good, cheap eateries.

Food stalls are a classic bargain food option, and an opportunity to eat with the locals. The stalls on **Phra Athit Road** in Banglampoo are no exception. A bit further south, a great deal for lunch awaits at **Thammasat University's** outdoor dining hall, where rice dishes go for 10B.

Those staying in the Samsen Road area should follow the road down to the river, where they will find the **Kaloang Home Kitchen** [2 Sri Ayuthaya Road, ☎ (02) 281 9228 or 282 7581]. Eat at this authentic Thai restaurant and you may never settle for bland, Westernized guest house fare again. The service is upscale, and the location right on the riverfront is hard to beat, yet you will find spending more than US$5 per person a challenge. Since the tables are mere feet from the river, I was a bit disconcerted to find "steamed local serpent head in chili soup" listed on the menu. But if there are local serpents in the water below, they are apparently tame. That is more than you can say for the curries, which are anything but tame. This restaurant is popular with the locals, who rave as much about the spicy food as about the flamboyantly gay waiters. You are likely to be the only *farang* here, which in my book is a good thing. Visa and MasterCard accepted.

Because of the language barrier, many travelers end up eating their meals at the guest houses. This strategy results in easy but plain dining. Try the food stalls for variety.

By bus, walk out of the airport building and turn left to find the bus stop. Air-conditioned bus No. 10 (or non-AC bus No. 59) will take you into the Khao San Road / Samsen Road area for 5B. Beware, chaos ensues on these buses during rush hour. Unfortunately, most flights from the USA arrive in Bangkok after 10pm, when the buses have stopped. At that time of night, your best bet is to share a cab with people you have met on the plane. Just outside customs, follow the driveway to the right, where you will spot a taxi stand, with cabs to Banglampoo running 200-300B. Demand that they use the meter; a negotiated flat fee will always be too much. If walking away from a negotiation, wait to start a new one until the first cabbie is out of sight. Otherwise, he may hand signal to the second cabbie, who will miraculously quote the exact same fare. Every guest house sells 50B tickets for the shuttle back to the airport, and the shuttle drivers sometimes know back roads that beat the traffic. Another way to avoid traffic is to take the train from downtown to the airport. The one-hour train ride is highly preferable to the 3-hour-plus crawl through Bangkok traffic that is your alternative. Ask the train conductor to tell you when you have arrived at the airport, since the train continues on. But an hour or so into the trip, you will see the airport terminal across the highway on the right side of the train.

UNIQUELY BANGKOK

Head down to Wat Po in the early morning so you can explore it before it is taken over by tourists. Once you have completed your explorations, head over to the wat's massage school to reap your rewards. Massage in Thailand has lots of sexual overtones, but on the temple grounds at Wat Po, you can get a nonsexual, traditional Thai massage for a moderate fee. The tables are outside in the open air, and the massages are given by students working to earn their licenses.

Bridges Worldwide

180-71 Vipavadeeragdisit Road

Donmuang International Airport

Bangkok, THAILAND

☎ (02) 533 4066

Fax 02/ 533 6179

Contact: Anan

Times to Call: 9:30am to 5:30pm

Type of Provider: Courier company

Areas of Specialty: Asia

DESTINATIONS	SAMPLE ROUND-TRIP FARE	FULL COACH FARE	LENGTH OF STAY
Singapore	3,000B	12,190B	14 days

Payment Methods: Cash, money order, personal check

Minimum Age: 18 years

In Business Since: 1989

Recommended Advance Reservations: 2 weeks

One-way tickets available. For 500B surcharge, your ticket can extend your stay to one year. Call to check on last-minute discounts and free flights.

Council Travel (Blue & White Travel)

108/12-13 Khao San Road

Banglampoo, 10200

Bangkok, THAILAND

☎ (02) 282 7705 or 282 0507

Fax 02/ 281 3792

Internet: http://members.tripod.com/~BLUEandWHITE/index.html

Times to Call: 9am to 5:30pm weekdays, 9am to 2pm Saturday

Type of Provider: Discount travel agent

Areas of Specialty: Worldwide student, youth, and budget travel

DESTINATIONS	SAMPLE ROUND-TRIP FARE	FULL COACH FARE
Hanoi	B6,700	B4,540
Ho Chi Minh	B6,700	B4,195
Hong Kong	B5,750	B8,720
Katmandu	B8,100	B13,865
Singapore	B3,600	B12,190

Payment Methods: Cash, money order, travelers check, Visa, MasterCard

In Business Since: 1947

(See the Council Travel listing on page 29 in the Chicago chapter for company background.)

From

Bangkok

GM Tour & Travel

273 Khao San Road

Bangkok 10200 THAILAND

☎ (02) 282 3979 or 280 3760

Fax 02/ 281 0642

Times to Call: 8:30am to 5pm

Type of Provider: Discount travel agency

Areas of Specialty: Worldwide

DESTINATIONS	SAMPLE ROUND-TRIP FARE	FULL COACH FARE
Frankfurt	42,500B	62,200B
London	41,000B	31,505B
New York	58,400B	84,910B
Singapore	4,500B	12,190B
Sydney	28,000B	48,450B

Payment Methods: Cash, money order, certified check, Visa, MasterCard, American Express

In Business Since: 1989

GM sells most of its tickets on Singapore Airlines, Lufthansa, EVA and China Air

Jupiter Air (Siam Trans International)

78 Kiatnakin Building

Bushlane, New Road

Bangkok 10500 THAILAND

☎ (02) 235 6741 or 235 6751

Fax 02/ 236 1042

Contact: Sirirat

From

Bangkok

Times to Call: 10am to 7pm

Type of Provider: Courier company

Areas of Specialty: Worldwide

DESTINATIONS	SAMPLE ROUND-TRIP FARE	FULL COACH FARE	LENGTH OF STAY
Hong Kong	4500B	8,720B	14 days
San Francisco	17,000B	48,590B	1 month

Payment Methods: Cash or check

In Business Since: 1988

Courier Duties on Return Trip: Yes

Recommended Advance Reservations: 2 weeks

Hong Kong is Jupiter Air's hub city. Thus it is sometimes possible to reserve a courier flight from Hong Kong to other Asian cities, such as Bangkok or Tokyo. Keep in mind that you must be back in Hong Kong in time for your return flight.

Additional offices in many of the hub cities listed in this book. Jupiter strongly favors repeat business.

Media International Travel & Trading

5/28 Soi Ngamduplee

Rama 4 Road

Bangkok 10120 THAILAND

☎ (02) 286 3870, or 287 1505

Fax 02/ 287 1505

Times to Call: 8:30am to 5pm

Type of Provider: Discount travel agency

Areas of Specialty: India, Japan, Nepal, Singapore

DESTINATIONS	SAMPLE ROUND-TRIP FARE	FULL COACH FARE
Bombay	11,500B	10,110B
London	26,000B	31,505B
New York	25,000B	84,910B
Singapore	4,100B	12,190B
Tokyo	20,000B	30,720B

Payment Methods: Cash, money order, certified check, Visa, MasterCard, American Express, JCB

In Business Since: 1981

Media gets some special volume-based discounts for flights on Japan Airlines. They are across the street from the Malaysia Hotel. All tickets must originate in Bangkok.

OBC Courier

Vanit Building #1, 16th Floor, Room 1605
1126/1 New Petchburi Road
Bangkok 10400 THAILAND
☎ (02) 255 8590 or 331 6396
Fax 02/ 255 8593
Contact: Jintana or Charlie

Times to Call: 10am to 7pm
Type of Provider: Courier company
Areas of Specialty: Worldwide

DESTINATIONS	SAMPLE ROUND-TRIP FARE	FULL COACH FARE	LENGTH OF STAY
Singapore	3500B	12,190B	1 to 14 days

Payment Methods: Cash or check
In Business Since: 1990
Courier Duties on Return Trip: Yes
Recommended Advance Reservations: 2 weeks

Oscar Tours

74-10 Petchburi Road, Suite 31
Bangkok 10400 THAILAND
☎ (02) 254 4515
Fax 02/ 253 7536
Contact: Rachanee

Times to Call: 9am to 5pm Monday to Saturday
Type of Provider: Consolidator
Areas of Specialty: Middle East and Europe

DESTINATIONS	SAMPLE ROUND-TRIP FARE	FULL COACH FARE
Dubai	call	19,025B
Frankfurt	call	62,200B

From	London	call	31,505B
Bangkok	Rome	call	58,520B
	Zurich	call	61,480B

Payment Methods: Cash, money order, certified check, personal check, Visa, MasterCard, American Express
In Business Since: 1991

Flights on Thai International to Dubai, connecting to Emirates Air flights to Europe. Their contract with the airlines does not allow them to print their prices, but the fares they quote over the telephone or in person will amaze you.

S.S. Travel Service

10/12-13 Convent Road
Bangkok 10200 THAILAND
☎ (02) 236 7188, or 236 0285
Fax 02/ 236 7186

Times to Call: 8:30am to 5pm
Type of Provider: Consolidator
Areas of Specialty: Worldwide

DESTINATIONS	SAMPLE ROUND-TRIP FARE	FULL COACH FARE
London	25,000B	31,505B
Los Angeles	20,000B	48,590B
New York	25,400B	84,910B
Paris	23,500B	62,200B
San Francisco	20,000B	48,590B

Payment Methods: Cash, money order, certified check, Visa, MasterCard, American Express
In Business Since: 1974

While S.S. does directly consolidate for certain airlines (Air India, Ethiopian Air, Indian Airlines, Royal Nepal Airlines), they can also buy from other consolidators to get good deals, especially to Europe and the US. The company started in a tiny Chinatown shop with one man, and has grown to over 100 employees. They will happily export tickets, but those tickets must originate in Bangkok. They also sell discounted business-class seats on many airlines.

STA Travel

Wall Street Tower Building,14th Floor, Room 1406
33 Surawong Road
Bangrak, Bangkok 10500 THAILAND
☎ (02) 233 2582
Fax 02/ 237 6005
Internet: http://www.sta-travel.com/

Times to Call: 8:30am to 5pm
Type of Provider: Discount travel agency
Areas of Specialty: Worldwide

DESTINATIONS	SAMPLE ROUND-TRIP FARE	FULL COACH FARE
London	25,500B	31,505B
Los Angeles	21,000B	48,590B
New York	25,400B	84,910B
Paris	23,500B	62,200B
Sydney	15,000B	48,450B

Payment Methods: Cash, money order, certified check, personal
check, Visa, MasterCard, American Express
In Business Since: 1975

STA is the world's largest travel organization for students and young,
independent travelers. They have 120 locations worldwide. Some of
their best fares require student ID or carry a maximum age.

Their tickets are highly flexible, usually good for one year, and require
no advance purchase. Date changes can be made at any office worldwide for $25; refunds cost only $75. Such flexible tickets are a wise
choice for travelers going on long trips without fully concrete itineraries. STA tickets are priced based on one-way tickets, which makes
it easy to book open-jaw flights.

Vista Travel Service

24/4 Khao San Road
Banglampoo, Bangkok
☎ (02) 280 0348
Fax 02/ 629 1028

Times to Call: 9am to 5pm

From	*Type of Provider:* Consolidator	
Bangkok	*Areas of Specialty:* Vietnam, Indochina, Japan, Europe, Australia	

DESTINATIONS	SAMPLE ROUND-TRIP FARE	FULL COACH FARE
London	19,100B	31,505B
Los Angeles	20,700B	48,590B
New York	29,200B	84,910B
Sydney	14,900B	48,450B

Payment Methods: Cash, money order, certified check, Visa, MasterCard, American Express

In Business Since: 1984

There is a surcharge for credit card transactions. They sell a lot of tickets on Vietnam Air, Burma Air, Air India, Air Egypt, Bangladesh Air (to Europe), Alitalia and Garuda (to Australia).

HONG KONG

CHAPTER 12

MARKET TRENDS

Hong Kong is one of Asia's most popular tourist destinations. During vacation periods, including Christmas, summer and especially Chinese New Year, all but the most expensive airline seats are nearly impossible to come by. Try to book your flight two to three months in advance if you plan to travel at these busy times. The Hong Kong market has caught on to the amazing deals available to couriers, most commonly on flights within Asia. You should call on the first day of the month in order to book a courier flight two to three months later.

To get a feel for the market, look for ads in the *South China Morning Post*. But beware, there are very occasional reports of bait-and-switch schemes, if not outright fraud, encountered by people doing business with Hong Kong consolidators. Use credit cards when possible, and pay only upon receipt of a confirmed ticket (call the airline first) when plastic is not accepted. Customs officials will usually accept "sufficient funds" in lieu of the onward tickets normally required to enter the country. Guest houses and hostels, while occasionally a bit grimy, are for the most part plentiful and tolerable.

STOPPING OVER IN HONG KONG

The "Pearl of the Orient," as Hong Kong is often called, is indeed a wondrous place to visit. From the time one enters Hong Kong airspace and endures the crazy, wide-eyed landing over Kowloon Tong, there is an adventure around every turn.

Hong Kong—which means "fragrant harbor" in Cantonese—is a city of endless contrasts. Just a ten-minute ride or a brisk hour's walk straight uphill from one of the world's most active financial centers, you can easily get lost in reverie on **Victoria Peak** (simply "The Peak" to locals). It's a must for any traveler, especially at night. Take the Peak Tram from Garden Road on Hong Kong Island. There is a free shuttle from the Star Ferry Terminal. The tram ride takes about 10 minutes each way and costs about HK$20 each for a round-trip ticket.

Public transportation is generally fast and easy. Buses, trams and the subway (called the Mass Transit Railway, or MTR) have frequent stops

TELEPHONE COUNTRY CODE:
(852)

CURRENCY:
Hong Kong Dollar
US$1 = HK$7.73
HK$1 = US$0.13

through the territory and are inexpensive. Be sure to carry a lot of change, though; in most cases exact change is required. Another tip for getting around involves the lobby of the **Kowloon Hotel**, which houses a computer that will print out in Chinese characters the names of the sights you hope to visit on a given day. Sure, the machine probably exists for hotel guests to use, but it is self-service, and it sure makes asking for directions easier.

Of course, the big question on the minds of all Hong Kong-bound tourists (and for that matter, Hong Kong residents) is what will happen when the British relinquish control in 1997. Changes have already begun, but there's still time to catch Hong Kong in its glory. The Hong Kong economy continues to grow by leaps and bounds, and if China follows up on its pledge of relative non-intervention, this growth will likely continue for years to come.

The green ferries of the Star Line shuttle back and forth between **Kowloon** and **Hong Kong Island**. For the cost of a cheap cup of coffee, you get a close-up of one of the most dramatic harbor cityscapes in the world. At the same time, the harbor itself is a chaotic whirlpool of cargo carriers, British warships, cruise liners, fishing sampans, junks and oar-driven dragon boats. By the time you arrive there the British may be gone, but the sampans will remain.

CHEAP SLEEPS

Lodgings in Hong Kong range from cheap and seedy to posh and expensive. Market trends show a reduction in the number of available hotel rooms because developers can use the land more lucratively for office space. Even some Hong Kong landmarks are now in danger. For the traveler, this means higher prices and less availability for any range of accommodation.

For the most part, it's best for budget-minded travelers going to Hong Kong to plan ahead. Hostels and guest houses fill up very quickly, and the time it takes to make a few phone calls will avoid the inconvenience of dragging your luggage around town searching for a place to lay your head.

One contact is the **Hong Kong Youth Hostels Association** (HKYHA, ☎ 2788 1638). For HK$60, they will sell IYHF cards and a member's handbook highlighting hostels in Hong Kong. Most hostels cost HK$25 a night and are closed between 10am and 4pm. Many have an 11pm curfew. Advance booking is required at some, but recommended at all locations.

Chungking Mansions
30 Nathan Road
Kowloon, HONG KONG

Seedy and decrepit, Chungking Mansions defies logic in its ability to attract international budget travelers. Yet for years it has been the quintessential meeting place of the backpacker set. Recent reports show an upsurge in crime here, due in large part to illegal immigration from the mainland. Even though every other guidebook recommends Chungking Mansions, we suggest that you attempt to find lodging elsewhere. Nonetheless, a stay in Chungking Mansions puts one right in the heart of Kowloon. Crowds, pollution and shops selling everything under the sun are quite abundant in this area. Prices are rising sharply of late, as the guest houses struggle to comply with new city codes.

Longtime residents of Hong Kong suggest staying in the upper or lower floors for quick exit to fresh air in case of fire. The following are some recommendations in "A" Block that meet these specifications: **The Traveler's Hostel** (☎ 2368 7710) on the 16th floor was renovated in the early 1990s and has relatively good security. This hostel has been popular for years, and is a good place to network with other travelers. Accommodations run HK$60-160 for dormitories, and double rooms with or without a bathroom. **Sky Guest House** (☎ 2368 3767), on the 3rd floor, is one of the cheapest and dirtiest places to stay in Hong Kong. Dormitory beds run about HK$40. The biggest plus, of course, is it's a very short walk up the stairs—and down.

Staying on the Kowloon side and moving up a bit on the price scale, the **Mirador Mansions** at 58 Nathan Road is a cleaner, smaller version of the notorious Chungking Mansions. The **Man Hing Lung Guest House** on the 14th floor (☎ 2722 0678) is very clean and has singles and doubles available for HK$160 per night. Management will match up single travelers, which will reduce the price to HK$80 each. All rooms have a private bath, air conditioning and television.

Hostels, guest houses and dormitories are not restricted to the Kowloon side of the harbor, however. They are plentiful on Hong Kong Island as well. A bit out of the way, but clean and quiet, the **Ma Wui Hall Youth Hostel** (☎ 2817 5715) comes highly recommended. With great harbor views from atop Mount Davis near Kennedy Town on the Western part of Hong Kong Island, the HK$25 nightly price tag is a great bargain. Getting there can be a bit rough: from the airport, take the A2 bus to Central, then change to the 5B or 47. From the bus stop, walk back 100 meters and look for the YHA sign and follow the road up the hill. There is a well-marked shortcut. The walk from the bus stop to the hostel takes about 30 minutes, so if you can't climb the hill with your baggage you may need to take a taxi to the top.

In the middle price range, the **Harbor View International House** (1 MacDonnell Road in Central, ☎ 802 0111) rents clean, comfortable doubles for HK$480–580, and is in a safe and relatively convenient location. The peak tram station is not far and the Central business district is a short walk down some very steep steps. The 12A bus, an air-conditioned double decker that stops near the hotel, is a quick, easy, and relatively inexpensive (about HK$4) way to get to the heart of Central.

CHEAP EATS

Temple Street Night Market

Hundreds of stalls are set up each night, mostly by vendors of bargain clothes, jewelry and other factory seconds. These vendors have to eat, so other vendors run food stalls at the north end of the market. Find a stall that looks popular, sit down, and point at whatever looks good. You can't find cheaper food this side of Marrakesh. Indian, Indonesian and Philippine cuisines complement the local Cantonese fare. Open approximately 8pm to 11pm. Recent reports have pickpockets plying their trade here (and in any other crowded place in the world), so be smart. Take the MTR to the Jordan Road Station, and follow the signs for the Temple Street Exit.

City Hall Dim Sum
City Hall Low Block
Edinburgh Place
Central, HONG KONG

Dim Sum (stuffed dumplings, usually fried or steamed) is one of Hong Kong's specialties—and the City Hall is among the locals' favorite places to sample it. It is traditionally served on trolleys. There's not a lot of English spoken here, so you just point at what you want as the trolleys cruise past you. Tables fill up and all the trolleys empty very fast, so it is best to arrive early—in most cases before 11am. No reservations, all major credit cards accepted, casual attire. Open 10am to 2pm.

The next two options are slightly more upscale:

The American Restaurant
20 Lockhart Road
Wanchai, HONG KONG
☎ 2527 1000

The American Restaurant (originally named to lure American sailors) is something of a Hong Kong tradition. It has been serving top-quality Peking cuisine at bargain-basement prices since just after World War II. Specialties include Peking Duck and Beggars Chicken (both dishes are a bit more expensive, but compared to the prices at most establishments here, a great value). Chili prawns on a sizzling plate are another excellent choice. Fixed-price meals are available at lunch. Reservations recommended, casual attire. Two can eat well here for HK$200. Lunch from 11am, dinner until 11:15pm. No credit cards.

Carrianna
2/F Hilton Tower, 96 Granville Road
Tsimshatsui East, Kowloon, HONG KONG
☎ 2724 4828

An excellent value for the local specialty—Chiu Chow cuisine. The high-priced luxury dishes such as Shark's Fin are to be avoided, but try the baby oysters in scrambled eggs. Some excellent dim sum dishes are also available. Casual dress. Lunch from 11:30am to 3pm, dinner from 5pm to 11:30pm. Credit cards accepted, reservations

153

recommended. Set meals available at lunch and dinner. Two people can eat too much for HK$300. There is a second location at 151 Gloucester Road in Wanchai.

TO & FROM THE AIRPORT

The Airbus airport shuttles depart from just outside the arrivals area, running every 15 minutes from 7am to midnight. There are several individual routes: the A1 goes to Tsimshatsui in Kowloon, passing the Chungking Mansions and going out to the Star Ferry. The A2 serves Wanchai, Central and the Macau Ferry Terminal. The A3 heads out to Causeway Bay. The Airbus stops at major hotels as well as posted bus stops, and costs HK$12-18.

UNIQUELY HONG KONG

The outlying islands present a host of adventures for travelers, and reveal a whole different side of Hong Kong. Most are accessible by ferry in under an hour. Ferry schedules are available at the Star Ferry terminal on both sides of the harbor.

Lantau Island offers several options. From the island's ferry terminal, you can take bus No. 2 to the **Po Lin Monastery**, home of a gigantic statue of Buddha and a wonderful hiking path. The bus ride is a white-knuckle affair along narrow, winding roads, but it's worth it. The hiking path—up toward Lantau Peak—is very steep and only recommended for those in excellent health. From the peak, the views of Lantau Harbor and back toward Buddha are certainly reward enough. Lunch at the monastery is vegetarian-style, since no meat is allowed on the grounds. Another option is to take bus No. 1 from the Lantau Ferry terminal, which goes to the **Tai O** fishing village. Step off the bus, and walk into old Hong Kong—the kind of place most travelers have only seen in black-and-white postcards.

Airtropolis Express

HONG KONG

☎ 2751 6186

Fax 2755 8467

Times to Call: 9am to 5:30pm
Type of Provider: Courier company
Areas of Specialty: Asia

DESTINATIONS	SAMPLE ROUND-TRIP FARE	FULL COACH FARE	LENGTH OF STAY
Jakarta	HK$2,800	HK$6,850	flexible
Kuala Lumpur	HK$2,600	HK$6,420	flexible
London	HK$5,200	HK$14,670	flexible
Singapore	HK$2,200	HK$5,820	flexible

Payment Methods: Cash only
Courier Duties on Return Trip: No
Minimum Age: 18 years
In Business Since: 1989
Recommended Advance Reservations: 2 weeks

Call to check on last-minute discounts. Return dates are flexible, and you can use all of your checked baggage allotment on the flight home.

Bridges Worldwide

Room 908, Pacific Trade Center
2 Kaihing Road
Kowloon Bay, HONG KONG
☎ 2305 1412 or 2305 1413
Fax 2795 8312
Contact: Jeanne

Times to Call: 9:30am to 5:30pm
Type of Provider: Courier company
Areas of Specialty: Worldwide

DESTINATIONS	SAMPLE ROUND-TRIP FARE	FULL COACH FARE	LENGTH OF STAY
Bangkok	HK$1,000	HK$4,120	up to 21 days
Bombay*	HK$3,200	HK$8,780	up to 30 days
London	HK$5,000	HK$14,670	up to 45 days

155

From

Hong Kong

| San Francisco | HK$4,500 | HK$13,380 | up to 1 year |
| Sydney | HK$6,800 | HK$13,880 | 6 to 60 days |

* An Indian passport is required for this flight.

Payment Methods: Cash, money order, personal check
Courier Duties on Return Trip: Yes
Minimum Age: 18 years
In Business Since: 1989
Recommended Advance Reservations: 3 months

One-way tickets are available to Bangkok, San Francisco and Sydney. There are two flights per day to Bangkok, which is convenient if you are traveling with a companion. Call to check on last-minute discounts and free flights! This company maintains a cancellation phone list. Flights on Canadian, Gulf Air, Qantas, and Thai Air.

Most flights allow you to bring 20 kilograms of checked luggage. The San Francisco flight allows checked luggage on the return portion only.

Hong Kong Student Travel (Sincerity Travel)

1812 Argyle Centre, Phase 1
688 Nathan Road
Kowloon, HONG KONG
☎ 2390 0421
Fax 2721 3269
Internet: http://www.sta-travel.com/

Times to Call: 10am to 7:30pm weekdays, 10am to 6:30pm Saturday, 12pm to 5pm Sunday
Type of Provider: Discount travel agency
Areas of Specialty: Worldwide

DESTINATIONS	SAMPLE ROUND-TRIP FARE	FULL COACH FARE
Bangkok	HK$1,900	HK$4,120
London	HK$6,150	HK$14,670
Los Angeles	HK$5,500	HK$11,680
New York	HK$7,600	HK$22,960
Sydney	HK$6,300	HK$13,380
Tokyo	HK$4,140	HK$6,320

Payment Methods: Cash, money order, certified check, personal check, Visa, MasterCard

In Business Since: 1975

HKST has several offices throughout Hong Kong, all of which are members of the STA Travel Network. STA is the world's largest travel organization for students and young, independent travelers. They have 120 locations worldwide. Some of their best fares require student ID or carry a maximum age.

Their tickets are highly flexible, usually good for one year, and require no advance purchase. Date changes can be made at any office worldwide for $25; refunds cost only $75. Such flexible tickets are a wise choice for travelers going on long trips without fully concrete itineraries. STA tickets are priced based on one-way travel, which makes it easy to book open-jaw flights.

Jupiter Air Ltd.

Room 1701, Tower One
China Hong Kong City
33 Canton Road
Kowloon, HONG KONG
☎ 2735 1946
Fax 2735 0450

Times to Call: 9am to 5:30pm weekdays, 9am to 1pm Saturday
Type of Provider: Courier company
Areas of Specialty: Worldwide

DESTINATIONS	SAMPLE ROUND-TRIP FARE	FULL COACH FARE	LENGTH OF STAY
Bangkok	HK$800	HK$4,120	up to 14 days
Chicago	HK$5,000	HK$14,820	up to 30 days
London	HK$5,000	HK$14,670	up to 30 days
Los Angeles	HK$3,800	HK$11,680	up to 30 days
New York	HK$5,500	HK$22,960	up to 30 days
Singapore	HK$2,100	HK$5,820	up to 30 days
Sydney	HK$6,500	HK$13,380	up to 30 days
Vancouver	HK$5,000	HK$12,520	up to 30 days

Payment Methods: Cash, money order, personal check

Deposit: Normally HK$1,000. No deposit for Sydney; HK$2,000 for Bangkok

Courier Duties on Return Trip: Yes

Minimum Age: 18 years

In Business Since: 1988

Call on the first day of the month, two months ahead of time, in order to reserve a flight. For example, for October flights you must call on August 1st. On August 2, there will be very few of these great deals left. At press time, there were two flights per day to New York. One-way tickets are available to Sydney for HK$3,800 and to Tokyo for HK$1,000. This company maintains a cancellation phone list.

The prices listed apply to the months of February, July, August and September. The rest of the year, tickets are about HK$500 cheaper. Current prices appear in ads in the *South China Morning Post.* Checked baggage is allowed on many flights.

Linehaul Express / Sophia Lai

Room 2209-B Tower One

33 Canton Road

Kowloon, HONG KONG

☎ 2735 2163, 2735 2167, or 2736 2769

Fax 2735 1372

Contact: Matthew Chan, Rosana Leung, Wendy To

Times to Call: 9:30am to 5:30pm

Type of Provider: Courier company

Areas of Specialty: Worldwide

DESTINATIONS	SAMPLE ROUND-TRIP FARE	FULL COACH FARE	LENGTH OF STAY
Bangkok	HK$1,600	HK$4,120	3 to 14 days
Frankfurt	HK$6,700	HK$22,810	10 to 30 days
London	HK$6,000	HK$14,670	7 to 30 days
Manchester	HK$6,500	n/a	7 to 30 days
Manila	HK$800	HK$2,840	3 to 10 days
Osaka	HK$2,500	HK$6,360	up to 30 days
Seoul	HK$1,700	HK$7,040	up to 30 days
Shanghai	HK$1,900	HK$3,020	up to 30 days
Singapore	HK$2,100	HK$5,820	4 to 30 days

Sydney	HK$5,800	HK$13,880	7 to 30 days	*From*
Taipei	HK$1,200	HK$3,000	4 to 30 days	*Hong Kong*
Tokyo	HK$2,300	HK$6,320	5 to 14 days	

Payment Methods: Cash, travelers' check, Visa
Deposit: HK$2,000
Courier Duties on Return Trip: Yes
Minimum Age: 18 years
In Business Since: 1989
Recommended Advance Reservations: 2 to 3 months

Because Linehaul Express is the general sales agent for Cathay Pacific Wholesale Courier, all flights are on Cathay Pacific Airlines. Additional offices are located in Frankfurt and London.

One-way tickets are available. Call to check on last-minute discounts. This company maintains a cancellation phone list. A flight from Hong Kong with a stopover in both Bangkok and Singapore runs HK$2,300.

Major Travel (Hong Kong) Co.

Room 301, Lap Fai Building
6-8 Pottinger Street
Central, HONG KONG
☎ 2526 9226
Fax 2521 6797

Times to Call: 9am to 5pm
Type of Provider: Consolidator
Areas of Specialty: Worldwide

DESTINATIONS	SAMPLE ROUND-TRIP FARE	FULL COACH FARE
Bangkok	HK$2,200	HK$4,120
London	HK$6,950	HK$14,670
Los Angeles	HK$6,100	HK$11,680
New York	HK$7,600	HK$22,960
Sydney	HK$6,900	HK$13,880

Payment Methods: Cash, money order, certified check, personal check, Visa, MasterCard, American Express
In Business Since: 1982

Prestige Travel

8th Floor, Jubilee Commercial Building

42-46 Gloucester Road

Wan Chai, HONG KONG

☎ 2528 6006

Fax 2861 2150

Times to Call: 9am to 6pm

Type of Provider: Consolidator

Areas of Specialty: Europe and Asia

DESTINATIONS	SAMPLE ROUND-TRIP FARE	FULL COACH FARE
Bangkok	HK$1,900	HK$4,120
London	HK$7,020	HK$14,670
Los Angeles	HK$6,800	HK$11,680
Paris	HK$7,600	HK$21,500
Sydney	HK$7,200	HK$13,880
Tokyo	HK$8,700	HK$6,320

Payment Methods: Cash, check, Visa, MasterCard

In Business Since: 1984

Prestige works with both business and student travelers. They have chosen to remain small in order to offer better service and lower prices.

Time Travel

16th Floor, A Block, Chungking Mansions

Kowloon, HONG KONG

☎ 2723 9993

Fax 2739 5413

Times to Call: 9am to 5pm

Type of Provider: Consolidator

Areas of Specialty: Worldwide

DESTINATIONS	SAMPLE ROUND-TRIP FARE	FULL COACH FARE
Bangkok	HK$1,780	HK$4,120
London	HK$6,800	HK$14,670
Los Angeles	HK$6,150	HK$11,680
New York	HK$7,250	HK$22,960

| Sydney | HK$6,750 | HK$13,380 | *From* |
| Tokyo | HK$5,800 | HK$6,320 | *Hong Kong* |

Payment Methods: Cash, check, Visa
In Business Since: 1979

This agency is part of the Traveler's Hostel in the Chungking Mansions, and comes highly recommended.

SINGAPORE

CHAPTER 13

MARKET TRENDS

Singapore used to be a major center of ticket exporting; now, Singapore agencies import tickets issued elsewhere. Times really have changed. It is important to note that the price for tickets in Singapore and Malaysia is often the same dollar amount; depending on the value of each currency, you may get a much better deal by buying in Malaysia. Garuda Indonesia airlines reliably offers some of the best deals out of Singapore.

But your best bet out of Singapore is catching a courier flight, usually to other Asian destinations, but sometimes to London. Pick up a copy of the *Straits Times* to get a feel for the latest airfares. Beware of the exit airport tax, for which you must reserve S$12 cash to pay at the airport on your way home. Customs officials will accept "sufficient funds" in lieu of the onward tickets normally required to enter the country.

STOPPING OVER IN SINGAPORE

Singapore is a well-functioning, thriving metropolis. One visitor refers to it as "Chicago on an island." Most activities for the visitor involve shopping or eating. Beaches and similar areas of natural beauty are harder to find.

Singapore is stiflingly clean, approaching dull, some would say. But beyond the tourist-ridden plazas of Orchard Road, those who stop to look will find a hidden charm that makes a visit worthwhile. Behind the skyscraper-laden Western facade of the commercial sector lies a strong Asian culture rooted in Confucian traditions. Venture into Chinatown or Little India to catch a glimpse of Singapore with its guard down.

TELEPHONE
COUNTRY CODE:

(65)

CURRENCY:
Singaporean Dollar
US$1 = S$1.40
S$1 = $0.71

The climate is consistently hot and sticky year-round. During the November–January monsoon season, Singapore is slightly cooler, albeit much wetter. The heat does not seem unbearable amidst the air-conditioned buildings, taxis, stores, buses and MRTs (Mass Rapid Transit subways). Like everything else in Singapore, public transit is clean and efficient.

Singapore is a prime example of redevelopment gone out of control.

Even the infamous Raffles Hotel was nearly demolished to make way for more office towers. Finding the need to modernize irresistible, developers decided to transform the rescued Raffles from an unpretentious colonial hotel into an opulent, super-luxurious operation. Drop in to try a Singapore Sling (which was first concocted here), but stay somewhere else unless you have a large inheritance to burn.

A note on bargaining: if a vendor asks, tell him you are staying at the youth hostel. Vendors are not asking out of friendly curiosity; they simply need to know how much money you have. They will quote much higher prices for shoppers saying at the Raffles than those staying at hostels. Bargaining is expected everywhere except in department stores. Tipping is not expected.

Oh, yeah. Obey the law in Singapore. Don't spit, don't litter, don't chew gum. Do use crosswalks, flush, and smile at the ubiquitous police. By meticulously conforming, you will prevent your trip from coming to, er, a painful end. . . .

CHEAP SLEEPS

Bencoolen Street is home to many of Singapore's best budget lodging opportunities. Conveniently located near the Queen Street Terminal, this neighborhood is also pleasantly far from the Orchard Road tourist traps.

Goh's Homestay
169 D Bencoolen Street, 6th Floor
Singapore
☎ 339 6561
Fax 339 8606

Basic, air-conditioned rooms. In the same building are the Hawaii Guest House on the 2nd floor, and Philip Choo's on the 3rd floor. Dorm rooms S$12, singles S$36, doubles S$46.

Hotel Bencoolen
47 Bencoolen Street
Singapore
☎ 336 0822
Fax 336 4384

In the moderate price category, this is a pleasant, small hotel. All rooms have A/C and private bath. Center rooms, either singles or doubles, cost S$94. Deluxe rooms are about S$10 more. Complimentary breakfast.

YMCA International House
1 Orchard Road
Singapore
☎ 337 3444
Fax 337 3140

If you must be in the middle of the Orchard Road madness, this is the cheap place to stay. The Y is a functional, practical, hotel-like place, with a rooftop swimming pool, billiards room and health club. All rooms have A/C and private baths. Dorm beds are S$23, singles are S$75, and doubles are S$85.

CHEAP EATS

Hawker centers are clearly a best buy. Working-class folks stop in for delicious, authentic fare in a food-stall atmosphere. Tourists do not frequent such establishments, but true travelers relish the opportunity to share a table with the locals. Order dishes from multiple, ethnically diverse stalls, depending on what looks good. Well-known hawker centers can be found at **The Satay Club** (on Queen Elizabeth Walk, a few blocks towards the waterfront from Raffles), **Paradiz Centre** (Selegie Road near Bencoolen), and **Newton Circus** (the trendy crowd congregates here at night, near Newton MTR stop).

Fatty's, now in a storefront on Albert Street near Bencoolen, serves up cheap but high-quality Cantonese fare. The jolly chef Fatty opened this place when the government decided that outdoor food stalls (including Fatty's) no longer fit the Official Plan for Albert Street. The change in locale has done nothing but improve his popularity.

TO & FROM THE AIRPORT

Catch bus No. 390 from Basement 2. Fare is S$1.30; exact change required. The ride to the city center takes about 45 minutes. Buses run every 15 minutes from 6am to 11:45pm. The bus will drop you off at the Queen Street Terminal on Rochor Road, which is a good area for budget lodgings. Bus No. 16 or 16/Express is another option, running from the airport to the corner of Bras Basah and Bencoolen Streets. Again, exact fare of S$1.30 is required. Large, unwieldy baggage is not allowed. This bus runs from 6am to midnight.

UNIQUELY SINGAPORE

Hidden Singapore is very well hidden; ask locals who look in the know for the latest word-of-mouth tips. One place to get away from the air conditioning (so as to regain an appreciation for it, of course) is the **Bukit Timah Nature Reserve** on Upper Bukit Timah Road. This sprawling expanse of primary jungle has predictably well-kept trails.

Air United

150 Orchard Road, Unit 73-70 Orchard Plaza

SINGAPORE 238841

☎ 735 7684

Fax 735 7584

Contact: Karen Ho

Times to Call: 9am to 5pm

Type of Provider: Courier company

Areas of Specialty: Worldwide

DESTINATIONS	SAMPLE ROUND-TRIP FARE	FULL COACH FARE	LENGTH OF STAY
Bangkok	S$220	S$1,041	up to 30 days
Hong Kong	S$450	S$1,560	up to 14 days
Los Angeles	S$800	S$3,035	up to 30 days
Manila	S$500	S$1,572	up to 30 days
San Francisco	S$800	S$3,035	up to 30 days

Payment Methods: Cash, check

Deposit: S$200

Courier Duties on Return Trip: Yes

Minimum Age: 18 years

In Business Since: 1989

Recommended Advance Reservations: 1 month

Call to check on last-minute discounts. All destinations allow 20 kilograms (one piece) of checked luggage.

Airtropolis Express

Fook Hai Building, Basement 1, B1-09

SINGAPORE

☎ 543 1934 or 538 1703

Fax 534 2604

Times to Call: 9am to 6pm

Type of Provider: Courier company

Areas of Specialty: Asia

DESTINATIONS	SAMPLE ROUND-TRIP FARE	FULL COACH FARE	LENGTH OF STAY
Bangkok	S$250	S$1,041	3 to 14 days

Payment Methods: Cash only
Courier Duties on Return Trip: Yes
Minimum Age: 18 years
In Business Since: 1989
Recommended Advance Reservations: 2 weeks

Call to check on last-minute discounts. Checked luggage allowed on return flight.

Bridges Worldwide

SATS Air Freight Terminal, Module 1A
Second Floor, Room 203
Changi Airport, Singapore 1781
☎ 545 4327
Fax 543 0258
Contact: Jumat

Times to Call: 9:30am to 5:30pm
Type of Provider: Courier company
Areas of Specialty: Worldwide

DESTINATIONS	SAMPLE ROUND-TRIP FARE	FULL COACH FARE	LENGTH OF STAY
Bangkok	S$200	S$1,041	up to 14 days

Payment Methods: Cash only
Courier Duties on Return Trip: Yes
Minimum Age: 18 years
In Business Since: 1989
Recommended Advance Reservations: 2 weeks

Call to check on last-minute discounts and free flights! This company maintains a cancellation phone list.

This flight allows you to bring 20 kilograms of carry-on luggage. Hong Kong, London, Manila, San Francisco and Sydney have been offered as courier destinations from Singapore in the past, and may be available again in the future.

CIEE Travel

110D Killiney Road

Tai Wah Building

Singapore 0923

☎ 738 7066

Fax 733 7421

Internet: http://www.ciee.org/cts/ctshome.htm

Times to Call: 9am to 5:30pm weekdays, 8:30am to 1pm Saturday

Type of Provider: Discount travel agent

Areas of Specialty: Worldwide

DESTINATIONS	SAMPLE ROUND-TRIP FARE	FULL COACH FARE
Bangkok	$S305	S$1,041
London	$S1,550	S$3,721
New York	$S2,100	S$5,279
Sydney	$S700	S$3,568

In Business Since: 1947

Payment Methods: Cash, money order, personal check, Visa, MasterCard, American Express

(See the Council Travel listing on page 29 in the Chicago chapter for company background.)

Gasi Travel

12 Devonshire Road

Singapore 0923

☎ 235 9900

Fax 738 3767

Times to Call: 9am to 5:30pm

Type of Provider: Consolidator

Areas of Specialty: Worldwide, including around-the-world

DESTINATIONS	SAMPLE ROUND-TRIP FARE	FULL COACH FARE
London	S$1,923	S$3,721
Los Angeles	S$1,700	S$3,035
New York	S$2,250	S$5,279
Paris	S$2,033	S$5,118
Sydney	S$1,288	S$3,568
Tokyo	S$1,571	S$2,573

Payment Methods: Cash, check, Visa

In Business Since: 1972

Gasi imports tickets from all over the world, and can get you some of the cheapest flights out of Singapore.

STA Travel

2-17 Orchard Parade Hotel

1 Tanglin Road

Singapore 247905

☎ 734 5681

Fax 737 2591

Internet: http://www.sta-travel.com/

Times to Call: 9am to 5pm weekdays, 9am to 1pm Saturday

Type of Provider: Discount travel agency

Areas of Specialty: Worldwide

DESTINATIONS	SAMPLE ROUND-TRIP FARE	FULL COACH FARE
Bangkok	S$300	S$1,041
London	S$1,070	S$3,721
Los Angeles	S$1,320	S$3,035
New York	S$1,420	S$5,279
Paris	S$1,480	S$5,118
Tokyo	S$1,018	S$2,573

Payment Methods: Cash, money order, certified check, personal check, Visa, MasterCard, American Express

In Business Since: 1975

There is a small surcharge for credit card transactions.

STA is the world's largest travel organization for students and young, independent travelers. They have 120 locations worldwide. Some of their best fares require student ID or carry a maximum age.

Their tickets are highly flexible, usually good for one year, and require no advance purchase. Date changes can be made at any office worldwide for $25; refunds cost only $75. Such flexible tickets are a wise choice for travelers going on long trips without fully concrete itineraries. STA tickets are priced based on one-way tickets, which makes it easy to book open-jaw flights.

TNT Skypak

12 Prince Edward Road, Unit 06-03

Podium B, Bestway Building

SINGAPORE 079212

☎ 222 7255

Fax 225 1654

Contact: Eileen

Times to Call: 8:30am to 5:30pm

Type of Provider: Courier company

Areas of Specialty: Worldwide

DESTINATIONS	SAMPLE ROUND-TRIP FARE	FULL COACH FARE	LENGTH OF STAY
Los Angeles	S$850	S$3,035	2 or 3 weeks

Payment Methods: Cash, personal check, Visa, MasterCard,
American Express

Courier Duties on Return Trip: Yes

Minimum Age: 18 years

In Business Since: 1991

Recommended Advance Reservations: 1 to 2 months

Call to check on last-minute discounts. This company also maintains
a standby phone list. First-time TNT couriers are sometimes allowed
to be on the standby list "if they are very sincere." All flights are on
Northwest Airlines.

SYDNEY, AUSTRALIA

MARKET TRENDS

For Those Headed Out of Australia
Standard airfares are painfully expensive in Australia. Even after deregulation, government capacity controls and pricey bilateral agreements set international fares so high, Aussies must often travel for an entire year or two at a time in order to justify the expense of airfare. Long distances within Australia combined with the small population make it difficult for new airlines to survive, let alone challenge the established airlines.

CHAPTER 14

Fortunately, there are courier flights out of Australia, and they are very poorly publicized. It shouldn't be difficult to book a courier flight for the dates you want at a price you won't believe. But your choices are currently limited to Auckland and London. California was a popular courier route, but couriers are no longer required by US customs. The determined might consider flying courier to Auckland, and picking up another courier flight from there to California. Call TNT Express – Auckland at (649) 275 0549 to investigate. Round-trip fares from Auckland to Los Angeles (with a free stopover or connection to Hawaii, San Francisco, Seattle or Vancouver) were running about NZ$1,400 at press time.

If you are unable to find a courier flight that suits your needs, your best bet is to shop around Sydney's consolidators. In addition to the listings in this chapter, cheap flights are always advertised in the weekend papers. Check out Saturday's *Melbourne Age* or the Sydney *Morning Herald*.

For Those Headed to Australia
You're best off purchasing internal airfares for Australia before you arrive. Your international round-trip ticket qualifies you for the air pass programs of both Ansett and Qantas, which offer domestic flights at fares dramatically cheaper than those otherwise available. But once you've arrived in the country/continent, it is too late to buy an air pass (for details, see Chapter 16: Air Pass Programs). Note that everyone except citizens of Australia and New Zealand needs a visa and an onward ticket to get into Australia.

TELEPHONE COUNTRY CODE:

(61)

CURRENCY:
Australian Dollar
US$1 = AU$1.25
AU$1 = $0.80

For bed and breakfasts, cruises, and tours, take advantage of stand-by rates. By waiting until the last minute, you can often get great deals if there is space available. Check the bulletin boards at each city's tourist office, or use the telephone book and call around. Savings of 50 percent or more are common.

STOPPING OVER IN SYDNEY

Situated around three spectacular harbors, Sydney was an obvious choice for one of Australia's first settlements. From humble beginnings as a convict colony to host city of the 2000 Olympic Games, Sydney has claimed an international reputation as one of the world's most beautiful cities.

If your mental image of Australia is of Ayers Rock and the Outback, Sydney will astonish you. It's a fast-paced, sophisticated and multicultural city. Sydney's own blend of natural beauty and outstanding architecture characterizes a city which has something for everyone.

Sydney Harbor sparkles. A blue sky creates an immaculate backdrop for viewing the city's unique skyline and world-famous harbor. The **Opera House** and bridge are best viewed from the water. Take the Manly Ferry from Circular Quay for AU$3.70. Enjoy the 30-minute ride, after which you will find yourself at one of Sydney's most famous beaches.

On the South Side, **Bondi Beach** is worth a visit for its fantastic selection of restaurants, cafés, and cosmopolitan beach life, especially on weekends.

The area between Circular Quay and the Harbor Bridge is known as The **Rocks,** and no tour of Sydney is complete without a walk around these historic streets. This is the site where the First Fleet chose to land and establish Britain's first outpost in Australia. Pick up a tour map from the **Rocks Visitors Centre** (104 George Street) and you can explore on foot.

CHEAP SLEEPS

The main concentration of hostels is in and around **Kings Cross**. Apart from being a lively red light district, Kings Cross is a melting pot of backpackers, 24-hour bars and unusual characters.

The Traveler's Rest
156 Victoria Street
Sydney, NSW 2011 AUSTRALIA
☎ (02) 358 4606

Dorm beds with common cooking facilities for AU$16. There are television in every room. Run by a family who lives on the premises. They pride themselves on being the cleanest hostel in Kings Cross. They are very helpful, and can even assist travelers who want to find work.

Eva's Backpackers
6 Orwell Street
Potts Point, NSW 2011 AUSTRALIA
☎ (02) 358 2185
Fax 02/ 358 3259

Dorm beds here run AU$17, and single rooms can be had for AU$20. The place is clean, and the staff is helpful and friendly.

For a more relaxed stay, close to the beach, try:

Coogee Beach Backpackers
94 Beach Street
Coogee, NSW 2034 AUSTRALIA
☎ (02) 665 7735
Fax 02/ 664 1258

Dorm beds for AU$16, or double rooms for $33. The friendly staff organizes a barbecue and volleyball game on the beach every Sunday.

Those looking for lodgings in the mid-priced category, consider:

Springfield Lodge
9 Springfield Avenue
Kings Cross, NSW 2011 AUSTRALIA
☎ (02) 358 3222
Fax 02/ 357 4742

This inexpensive small motel boasts a great central location in Kings Cross. Singles with bath run AU$44, doubles with bath are AU$49. The rooms feature polished wood floors, and offer individual sinks, coffeemakers and mini-refrigerators. The clientele is mostly small-town Australians.

CHEAP EATS

If you have the time to sample a few cafés and restaurants, invest in the thorough **Cheap Eats Guide** for AU$8.95, available from most news agencies.

Budget travelers will have little trouble finding cheap meals in the Kings Cross area. Many restaurants are geared towards them. Stroll along Darlinghurst Road or Victoria Street and you will come across a variety of cafés and take-out restaurants.

For cheap Italian food, bustling breakfasts, and a lively street scene, head to **Stanley Street**, East Sydney. One of the best restaurants is **Bill and Toni's** (74 King Street), where huge servings are the rule. Newtown has Sydney's best selection of inexpensive cafés and restaurants aimed at a student budget. **El Bamsa** at 233 King has the best coffee. **Café Stromboli**'s glass-roofed courtyard is an oasis of serenity at 134 King.

TO & FROM THE AIRPORT

All of the hostels listed above have an airport pickup service. Check the board and use the free telephone at the airport. Also, the No. 300 Airport Express bus runs from the airport to Central Station, Circular Quay, and Kings Cross every 20 minutes for AU$5, or AU$8 round trip if you plan ahead (times 6am to 11pm). From the airport, the No. 300 departs from the International Terminal.

UNIQUELY SYDNEY

Art fans will fall in love with **Paddington**, a hip, inner-city neighborhood where most of Sydney's galleries thrive in the midst of newly renovated terraces and classy pubs. Check out the arts-and-craft market held every Saturday at the corner of Newcombe and Oxford Streets.

Stretching from Paddington back towards the city is **Oxford Street**. In late February, Oxford Street explodes into action with Sydney's gay and lesbian Mardi Gras. The rest of the year, this area offers a vast array of pubs and clubs which draws a hip, mixed crowd. **The Freezer** at 11 Oxford Street has the latest dance mixes and draws a younger clientele.

To escape the inner city, the closest beach is in **Bondi**. Take bus No. 380 or 382 from Circular Quay. Sunday is the best day to visit if you enjoy promenading along waterfronts, dodging roller bladers, and listening to South American drummers and other buskers. Reggae bands play at the **Surf Pavilion** in the afternoons, further contributing to the cosmopolitan mayhem of Bondi Beach. For better surfing and more secluded beaches, take the bus from Manly Wharf towards Palm Beach (along the Northern Peninsula), stopping at Whale or Bungan beaches.

Jupiter Air

Street Address: Unit 6 / 154 Oriordan Street
Mailing Address: PO Box 224
Mascot, NSW 2020 AUSTRALIA
☎ (02) 317 2230
Fax 02/ 317 2113 or 317 3175
Contact: Robert or Sandra

Times to Call: 9am to 4pm Monday through Thursday
Type of Provider: Courier company
Areas of Specialty: Worldwide

DESTINATIONS	SAMPLE ROUND-TRIP FARE	FULL COACH FARE	LENGTH OF STAY
Auckland	AU$250	AU$679	7 to 10 days
London	AU$1,600	AU$2,599	up to 2 mos.

Payment Methods: Cash, bank check, personal check
Courier Duties on Return Trip: Yes
In Business Since: 1988
Recommended Advance Reservations: 1 to 3 months
Luggage: One checked bag plus carry-ons

London flights can be booked from either Melbourne or Sydney. One-way tickets are sometimes available. Flights are substantially pricier in high season, rising to about AU$1,800 return for London (but dropping as low as AU$1,100 in low season). The company stresses that the fares quoted above are only samples, and that prices are always changing. Jupiter Air is now the biggest courier company operating out of Australia. They cannot respond to unsolicited faxes, so contact them by telephone.

Phil Travel

6th Floor
105 Pitt Street
Sydney, 2000 AUSTRALIA
☎ (02) 232 5677
Fax 02/ 235 3142
Internet: philt@world.net, http://www.airdiscounter.com/

Times to Call: 9am to 5pm
Type of Provider: Discount travel agency

DESTINATIONS	SAMPLE ROUND-TRIP FARE	FULL COACH FARE
Bangkok	AU$735	AU$1,399
London	AU$1,460	AU$2,599
Los Angeles	AU$1,490	AU$2,513
New York	AU$1,630	AU$3,389
Paris	AU$1,460	AU$2,599
Tokyo	AU$1,080	AU$2,099

Payment Methods: Cash, Visa, MasterCard, American Express
In Business Since: 1984

Clients who are serious about getting the cheapest available air tickets are supplied with a market research form. Phil Travel is so confident that they can get you the cheapest fare, they encourage you to fill out the form and use it to shop around at other agencies. If you find a quote that they cannot match or better, they will give you AU$50 upon proof of purchase. Around the world fares start at AU$1,590.

Student Travel Australia (STA)
855 George Street
Sydney, NSW 2007 AUSTRALIA
☎ (02) 212 1255
Fax 02/ 281 4183
Internet: http://www.sta-travel.com/

Times to Call: 9am to 5pm
Type of Provider: Discount travel agency
Areas of Specialty: Worldwide

DESTINATIONS	SAMPLE ROUND-TRIP FARE	FULL COACH FARE
Bangkok	AU$750	AU$1,399
London	AU$1,630	AU$2,599
Los Angeles	AU$1,495	AU$2,513
New York	AU$2,135	AU$3,389
Paris	AU$1,630	AU$2,599
Tel Aviv	AU$1,780	n/a
Tokyo	AU$1,220	AU$2,099

Payment Methods: Cash, Visa, MasterCard, American Express

In Business Since: 1975

STA is the world's largest travel organization for students and young, independent travelers. They have 120 locations worldwide, including several in Sydney and Melbourne. Some of their best fares require student ID or carry a maximum age. If you need a student or youth card, they can issue one for you. It can get you into the Acropolis for free, saving AU$12.

Their tickets are highly flexible, usually good for one year, and require no advance purchase. Date changes can be made at any office worldwide for $25; refunds cost only $75. Such flexible tickets are a wise choice for travelers going on long trips without fully concrete itineraries. STA tickets are priced based on one-way tickets, which makes it easy to book open-jaw flights.

Sydney Flight Centre
Shop 524
Gateway Quay Side
1 MacQuarie Street
Sydney 2000 AUSTRALIA
☎ (02) 241 2422
Fax 02/ 241 4113

Times to Call: 9am to 5pm
Type of Provider: Consolidator
Areas of Specialty: Worldwide

DESTINATIONS	SAMPLE ROUND-TRIP FARE	FULL COACH FARE
Bangkok	AU$760	AU$1,399
London	AU$1,540	AU$2,599
Los Angeles	AU$1,380	AU$2,513
New York	AU$1,670	AU$3,389
Paris	AU$1,540	AU$2,599
Tel Aviv	AU$1,670	n/a
Tokyo	AU$1,120	AU$2,099

Payment Methods: Cash, money order, personal check
In Business Since: 1980

Consistently one of the cheapest travel agencies in Sydney, with offices all over Australia. Call ☎ (02) 131 600 to speak to the office nearest you.

The company motto is, "we guarantee to beat any genuine quoted price."

The Flight Centre operates many smaller offices, which gives them good buying power while still allowing for very personal service.

TNT Express Worldwide
280 Coward Street
PO Box 351
Mascot, NSW 2020 AUSTRALIA
☎ (02) 317 7717
Fax 02/ 669 3152
Contact: Lisa

Times to Call: 9am to 5:30pm
Type of Provider: Courier company
Areas of Specialty: New Zealand

DESTINATIONS	SAMPLE ROUND-TRIP FARE	FULL COACH FARE	LENGTH OF STAY
Auckland	AU$350	AU$679	up to 6 mos

Payment Methods: Cash, bank check, personal check
In Business Since: 1989
Courier Duties on Return Trip: No
Recommended Advance Reservations: 6 to 8 weeks for confirmed seat
Luggage: Varies

Two to three months before you plan to travel, call, listen to the recording, and leave your name and address. An application form with thorough details will be sent to you. You must complete the application before you can book. Return flight can be from Auckland, Christchurch, or Wellington. One-way flights available for AU$227.

TOKYO, JAPAN

CHAPTER *15*

MARKET TRENDS

Tokyo is one of the worst places in the world to buy air travel (second only to Saudi Arabia). The combination of high incomes, expense accounts, and government enforcement of IATA fares makes air travel pricey. So why even list Tokyo in a book on budget airfares? Because if you lack insider knowledge in this market, you are doomed to pay through the nose for air travel.

Try to have an onward ticket before you arrive in Japan, or buy your ticket abroad from a San Francisco or London consolidator and have it mailed to you. (Most foreign tourists need a confirmed onward ticket to get into Japan in the first place.) Courier flights offer genuinely good deals, but you do have to plan ahead. Other than joining the U.S. military, courier flights are the only way to fly cheaply out of Japan. If you can't fly courier, the consolidators listed for Tokyo will give you the best prices available, but that is not saying much. You may also find some ads for discounted tickets in the *Tokyo Journal*.

If you plan to visit parts of Japan beyond Tokyo, the cheapest (but not exactly cheap) way to do it is by train. To make train travel here more affordable, you should consider buying a railpass before you arrive. With such a pass, you can travel as much as you want for seven days for under US$300. If you wait until you get there, a single round trip from Tokyo to Kyoto will cost you US$260.

STOPPING OVER IN TOKYO

Tokyo is a lively if overpopulated city that sprawls like Los Angeles. Unlike Los Angeles, however, most places of interest to travelers can be found inside the ring of the Japan Railways Yamanote line, which circles central Tokyo. Shopping and nightlife are easy to find. Surprisingly, you can also find several historic sites nestled within the starkly modern terrain. Check out the **Senso-ji Temple** in Asakusa, the **Meiji Shrine** across from Harajuku, and the **Imperial Palace**, at the green line's Nijubashimae Station.

TELEPHONE COUNTRY CODE:

(81)

CURRENCY:

Yen

US$1 = ¥105

¥1 = $0.01

To find out what's going on in town, pick up a copy of the English-language weeklies *Tokyo Journal* or *Tokyo Time Out*. Orientation in the city is easy. All you need is a subway map, since the entire city is organized around its subway stations. A full street map of the city would be overwhelming. Average subway trips cost ¥120 to ¥200; you pay at the turnstiles. Whenever you get lost (and you will get lost), stop and ask for directions from one of the street-corner police kiosks, known as *kobans*. Or inquire at Tokyo's **Tourist Information Center,** near Yurakucho Station in Hibiya [☎ (03) 3502 1461].

Ginza is the upscale shopping district; technophiles will love Sony headquarters, where they can browse through several floors of the latest gadgetry. When hunger strikes, pop down into the Ginza train station, where a bowl of curry rice with egg on top will set you back a mere ¥280.

Young travelers may find **Shinjuku**'s maze of dazzling neon more interesting. In addition to Tokyo's red light and gay districts, Shinjuku boasts some of the trendiest nightclubs, clothing stores, and a collection of electronics bazaars. If you can hear them over the racket of the *pachinko* parlors, the live bands that perform in the park at the station play everything from jazz to rap. Also near Shinjuku Station is the **Sumitomo Building**, which you can scale for a great view of the city.

In terms of nightlife, **Roppongi** is home to the outrageously expensive international disco and yuppie scene, on the Hibiya line. Look for the famous two-story-high King Kong hanging off the side of the Hard Rock Cafe. The only free club in the area is nearby **Gas Panic,** hidden behind a red steel door (just past the Mr. Donut—ask for directions, as this place is well known). In the same area, **Club Buzz** is a popular techno dance place. Clubs generally charge a cover of ¥4,000 to ¥8,000, although women sometimes get in for half price. The pink **Almond Restaurant** marks the train station, and is a favorite meeting place for those bound for the Roppongi scene.

The more moderate **Shibuya** digs will still set back your pocketbook a bit, but the area is lively and worth the splurge. There certainly are sleazy clubs looking to fleece tourists in this neighborhood, so avoid the places that try to pull you in, and ask about covers and minimums. In general, Shibuya (Yamanote line) is the young alternative to the red lights and serious, traditional bars of Ginza and Shinjuku. The area is literally overflowing with youth and *gaijin* (foreigners).

Next to Shibuya, **Harajuku** can best be described as "teeny-bopper land." Come see all the latest adolescent fashions; bell bottoms are hot as of this writing. On Sundays, countless amateur musicians set up shop on the sidewalks.

CHEAP SLEEPS

Few things are cheap in Japan. Accommodations are no exception. Even the YMCA is expensive! Your best budget option is the **Tokyo International Youth Hostel** [18-F Central Plaza Building, 1-1 Kagura-kashi, Shinjuku, Tokyo, JAPAN; ☎ (03) 3235 1107], in the tall glass building outside Iidabashi Station. Dorm beds run about ¥2500 a night.

Ryokan are small, traditional Japanese hotels, complete with tatami mats and futons. The **Kimi Ryokan** [☎ (03) 3971 3766] has gained quite a following among travelers, though it can be a bit tricky to find. Go left at the eastern exit of Ikebukuro Station. Stop at the police koban on the corner, and ask the officer on duty for directions. Singles run ¥3,000 and up; doubles start at ¥5,000. Remember to swap your shoes for the provided slippers upon entering the ryokan, and to remove even the slippers before stepping on the *tatami* in your room. Some ryokans do not accept foreign guests because foreigners often do not understand the customs. If meals are served, expect the schedule to be rather firm.

You may want to stay in a *minshuku,* a small, family-run inn that can be cheaper than a ryokan, and is the Japanese equivalent of a bed and breakfast. For a list of Japanese lodgings including minshuku, contact the **Welcome Inn Reservation Center** in Tokyo at (03) 3211 4201, or fax them at (03) 3211 9009. Two meals are usually included, and prices run about ¥4,000 a person. You make your own bed and bring your own towel.

Other budget options include the uniquely Japanese "capsule hotels." These male-only cubicles can be found at train stations and airports. For ¥4,000, you get a locker-like (or coffin-like, depending upon your perspective) space, about one meter high and two meters

long, with a bed and a television. Crawl in and get comfortable! One
example is the **Ikebukuro Puraza** [☎ (03) 3590 7770], just outside
Ikebukuro Station.

If you plan to stay for more than a few days, a *gaijin* house is the cheapest way to go. Prices start around ¥1500 a night. Both the Tourist Information Center and the weekly magazines have contact information.

CHEAP EATS

Inexpensive restaurants can be found in the basements of most Japanese department stores. Try the one in **Takashimaya**, a large department store near the main shopping district of Ginza, for a basic lunch for about ¥600. This is the kind of place where the Japanese office workers eat, and that's always a good sign for budget travelers. The top three stories of the **Sumitomo Building** (see above) also house working-class restaurants.

A cheap and filling way to eat lunch or dinner on the run is to buy a *bento* (meal in a box) in supermarkets and convenience stores. You can find bentos for about ¥500.

Near the Meguro JR station, **Tonki** [1-1-2 Shimo-Meguro, ☎ (03) 3491 9928] draws a huge local following. The people in line are waiting for *tonkatsu,* the deep-fried pork cutlet and fixings that made this place famous. Expect a 15-minute wait to get a table in this frill-free, family-run treasure. No reservations, credit cards accepted, meals from ¥1,500.

In the same neighborhood, **Mekong** [Koyo Building 2-F, 2-16-4 Kamiosaki, Shinagawa-ku, ☎ (03) 3442 6664] is a good Southeast Asian restaurant. Spicy Cambodian, Thai, and Vietnamese dishes trail steam all the way from the kitchen to your vinyl-covered table. English menus, reservations accepted.

Noodle bars, yakitori shops, and curry-rice stalls are also good bets for budget eats. Look in the corridors of all major train stations. For example, below the train tracks between Yurakucho Station and Shimbashi is a collection of at least 50 such stalls. At ¥700, ramen can be much more filling than other sometimes dainty Japanese meals.

Shakey's Pizza won't help you assimilate, but you can gorge yourself on their all-you-can-eat lunch specials from 11am to 2pm.

TO & FROM THE AIRPORT

Many trains announce the stops in both English and Japanese, or post
signs in both languages inside each station. The fastest and cheapest
way to move to and from Narita Airport is by train. Take the Keisei
Limited Express to Ueno Park (¥1,800 one way), where you can connect with the subway system.

UNIQUELY TOKYO

It is said that in order to understand the Japanese you must bathe
with them. They have made an art form of bathing, and a visit to a
traditional public bath house can be an eye-opening experience. (Do
be careful not to confuse bath houses with the entirely different experience of *sopurando,* or "soap-lands.") These single-sex, communal
bathhouses, known as *sento,* are places that men go to relax with the
guys, and women with women.

The first difference between western and Japanese baths is the purpose: the goal is to soak, gossip and tell jokes, not to get clean. In
fact, you must scrupulously clean yourself with soap and water while
sitting on a stool outside the bath before you climb in. Bathers sometimes wash each other's backs and rinse each other off. Avoid getting
soap into the bath itself.

Once inside the bath, you may find the Japanese people suddenly
daring; they may laugh, gesture, make surprisingly blunt comments
or ask very personal questions. Remember that you can and should
joke and query right back. Smile, have fun, don't take anything too
seriously, and you are likely to leave the bath relaxed, with a whole
new perspective on the Japanese.

You can find a sento in just about any residential neighborhood. Ask
your innkeeper to point you towards a particularly good one. Most
are fairly basic, but a few have themes (the "Jungle" sento,
"Amusements" sento, etc.) **Sento Tsubameyu** [3-14-5 Ueno, Taitou-
ku] is a good introduction to these Japanese baths. The sento is open
from 6am to midnight, and is closed only on Monday. Consider arriv-

ing right at opening time, which is when the local morning bathers' association meets here.

From Tokyo

Council Travel

Sanno Grand Building, Room 102

2-14-2 Nagata-Cho

Chiyoda-Ku, Tokyo 100 JAPAN

☎ (03) 3581 5517

Fax 03/ 3581 5519

Internet: http://www.ciee.org/cts/ctshome.htm

Times to Call: 9:30am to 5:30pm

Type of Provider: Discount travel agent

Areas of Specialty: Worldwide

DESTINATIONS	SAMPLE ROUND-TRIP FARE	FULL COACH FARE
London	¥115,000	¥381,000
Los Angeles	¥90,000	¥210,000
New York	¥110,000	¥398,000
Sydney	¥120,000	¥335,500

In Business Since: 1947

Payment Methods: Cash, bank transfer

The Japanese branch of Council Travel does not handle intra-Asian flights.

(See the Council Travel listing on page 29 in the Chicago chapter for company background.)

Fastlink Express

654-207 Nanaei, Tomisato-Machi, Inba-Gun

Chiba 286-02 JAPAN

☎ (04) 7691 2895

Fax 04/ 7691 0313

Contact: Mr. Kukinono or Mr. Obara

Times to Call: 9am to 5pm

Type of Provider: Courier company

Areas of Specialty: Asia

DESTINATIONS	SAMPLE ROUND-TRIP FARE	FULL COACH FARE	LENGTH OF STAY
Bangkok	¥30,000	¥95,000	up to 3 mos
Hong Kong	¥30,000	¥84,000	up to 3 mos
Singapore	¥40,000	¥105,000	up to 3 mos

Payment Methods: Cash, bank transfer
Courier Duties on Return Trip: No
Minimum Age: 18 years
In Business Since: 1996
Recommended Advance Reservations: 3 months

STA Travel

4th Floor, Nukariya Building
1-16-20, Minami-Ikebukuro
Toshima-Ku, Tokyo 171 JAPAN
☎ (03) 5391 2922
Fax 03/ 5391 2923
Internet: http://www.sta-travel.com/

Times to Call: 9am to 5pm
Type of Provider: Discount travel agency
Areas of Specialty: Worldwide

DESTINATIONS	SAMPLE ROUND-TRIP FARE	FULL COACH FARE
Bangkok	¥79,000	¥95,000
London	¥92,000	¥381,000
Los Angeles	¥66,000	¥210,000
New York	¥109,000	¥398,000
Paris	¥92,000	¥381,000

Payment Methods: Cash, money order, certified check, personal
check, Visa, MasterCard, American Express
In Business Since: 1975

STA is the world's largest travel organization for students and young,
independent travelers. They have 120 locations worldwide. Some of
their best fares require student ID, or carry a maximum age.

Their tickets are highly flexible, usually good for one year, and require
no advance purchase. Date changes can be made at any office
worldwide for $25; refunds cost only $75. Such flexible tickets are a
wise choice for travelers going on long trips without fully concrete
itineraries. STA tickets are priced based on one-way tickets, which
makes it easy to book open-jaw flights.

Wholesale Courier

Tsumatsu Building, Second Floor

2-0-10 Hiyoshidai, Tomisato Inba-Gun

Chiba 286-02 JAPAN

℡ (04) 76 92 03 11

Fax 04/ 76 92 03 09

Contact: Mr. Endo

Times to Call: 9am to 6:30pm; closed for lunch 12pm to 1pm

Type of Provider: Courier company

Areas of Specialty: Asia

DESTINATIONS	SAMPLE ROUND-TRIP FARE	FULL COACH FARE	LENGTH OF STAY
Bangkok	¥35,000	¥95,000	up to 6 mos.
Hong Kong	¥30,000	¥84,000	up to 6 mos.
Singapore	¥35,000	¥105,000	up to 6 mos.

Payment Methods: Cash, bank transfer

Courier Duties on Return Trip: No

Minimum Age: 18 years

In Business Since: 1986

Recommended Advance Reservations: 3 months

These flights have gotten popular, so it is best to call a full three months in advance. If you cannot book far ahead, call to check on last-minute discounts, which can drop to ¥10,000. This company maintains a cancellation phone list for existing customers. All flights are on Northwest Airlines. Mr. Endo is often reachable about 6pm Tokyo time.

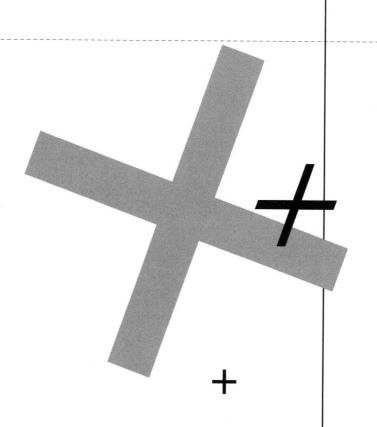

Air Pass Programs

If you plan to travel extensively in a large country or region, the air pass option is worth looking into. Air pass programs offer the convenience and speed of air travel at a price that can often be competitive with land-based transportation. When you factor in the value of your time, flying may offer a clearly superior alternative.

A few air pass programs operate just like Eurail tickets, good for unlimited travel during a certain period of time. Typically, however, these programs offer the traveler a booklet of coupons, where each coupon is valid for one flight segment. In some cases, the passes are valid for travel anywhere an airline flies in a particular country, as in the case of American Airlines' Visit USA pass. In other cases, several airlines cooperate to offer a program that covers several countries in a region. For example, the Euroflyer Pass offers flights throughout Europe, courtesy of an agreement between Sabena, Air Inter, CSA and Air France.

These programs usually require that you purchase your air pass before you arrive in the region; American Airlines' Visit USA pass, for example, cannot be purchased in the United States. Note that many air passes can be used by citizens of the country being visited, as long as the passes themselves are purchase abroad. Furthermore, some programs restrict air pass sales to travelers who purchased their international ticket on the sponsoring airline.

Other air passes can be bought once in the country, and by residents of that country. However, these passes are almost always available only to certain groups. Senior passes (usually for those age 62 and over) are the most common category. Most domestic US airlines offer such deals, although the best bargains seem to be on America West, Continental and TWA. There is usually no minimum stay requirement, and travelers usually earn frequent-flyer miles. TWA is also the only airline to offer student passes for travel within the US. See the listings below for details.

It is wise to ask whether flights that connect through a non-destination airport require only one coupon (as they should), or two coupons (as they sometimes do). This is especially true with passes that cover several countries. If to fly from Rome to Zurich you must use two coupons and fly through Amsterdam, using an air pass may be a poor investment of both time and money.

In general, airlines price these passes differently depending on the departure point of the traveler's international ticket. There are typically three price levels: passes are cheapest when purchased in the Third World, more expensive when purchased in Europe or the US, and most expensive when purchased in Japan.

Some programs allow you to buy exactly the number of coupons you need, while others have a minimum and/or a maximum. Most companies will allow you to return unused coupons for a refund, but check with individual airlines before you make your purchase. These coupons offer the best value when used for longer flights, or flights involving cities where lack of competition has kept fares high. For shorter flights, a regular ticket on a low-fare airline may be a better deal.

Telephone numbers provided are the direct, toll-free air pass hotlines for each airline's United States operations. Elsewhere in the world, call the main telephone number for the appropriate airline in your country. Unless otherwise specified, prices are listed in U.S. dollars.

AFRICA

Royal Air Moroc, ☎ (800) 344 6726
Discover Morocco

This simple air pass program offers travelers four coupons for $149, or six coupons for $169. All coupons must be used within six months of the first flight.

South African Airways, ☎ (800) 722 9675
Africa Explorer

This rather restrictive and finicky program prices each flight segment differently. Travelers can buy a minimum of four and a maximum of eight coupons, which must be used within 30 days. You must purchase an international flight on any airline in order to qualify. There is a 25 percent cancellation charge. The price quoted on a sample itinerary of Johannesburg–Cape Town–Port Elizabeth–Durban–Johannesburg was $320. To add a flight from Johannesburg to Nairobi and back costs an additional $541.

Air India, ☎ (800) 223 7776
Discover India

This program operates in conjunction with Indian Air, and offers unlimited flights during a 21-day period for $400. The period starts the day of your first domestic flight. Travelers may not revisit a city except in order to make a flight connection.

Garuda Indonesian Airways, ☎ (800) 342 7832
Visit Indonesia

These coupons run $100 apiece. You can buy anywhere from three to ten coupons, and must use all of them within 60 days. Flights must start in Bali, Jakarta or Medan. You use one ticket per destination, regardless of the number of connections required.

Thai Airways International, ☎ (800) 426 5204
Discover Thailand

This pass must be purchased in the United States. It offers four flight coupons for $239, with up to four additional coupons for $50 each. All coupons must be used within 60 days of the first flight. You must confirm the date and destination of your first flight and set your itinerary (with open dates) in advance.

AUSTRALIA

Ansett Airlines, ☎ (800) 366 1300
Visit Australia Pass

Pass must be purchased before arrival in Australia, in conjunction with an international flight. Additional coupons can be purchased once in Australia at any Ansett or EastWest ticketing location. Not available in Japan. In North America, you can buy a minimum of four and a maximum of eight coupons per pass. Outside North America, the minimum is only two coupons. Round-trip, circle-trip, and open-jaw flights are permitted. The Exclusive Pass (excluding Western Australian cities) costs AU$640 for four coupons, AU$160 for each additional coupon. The Inclusive Pass (including all Australian cities) runs AU$740 for four coupons, AU$210 for each additional coupon.

Qantas Airlines, ☎ (800) 227 4500
Australia Explorer Pass

Much like Ansett's pass, this program has different price structures depending on the zone in which the pass holder seeks to travel. Dates and destinations can be left open. Purchase the pass in conjunction with an international ticket from anywhere in the Western Hemisphere. The minimum book of four coupons costs $440, or $554 including flights to Perth, Ayers Rock, Alice Springs or the outer islands. Additional coupons cost $121 each (or $146 for the outlying destinations). Travelers may purchase up to eight coupons, and the last four coupons can be bought in Australia. You can reserve seats ahead of time, or just show up at the airport and take your chances.

EUROPE

Air France, ☎ (800) 237 2747
Euroflyer Pass

This pass is a result of a cooperative deal between Air France, Air Inter, CSA, and Sabena. Coupons cost $120 each, and are valid for any European flight on any of the partner airlines. The pass has a 7-day minimum and a 60-day maximum. To qualify, you must purchase the pass in conjunction with a USA–Paris ticket. You may purchase anywhere from three to nine coupons.

British Airways, ☎ (800) 247 9297
Europe Air Pass

Minimum of three coupons and used over at least seven days, with no maximums. All flights are on British Airways, Air Gibraltar, TAT (France) or Deutsche BA. Pass must start or end in the UK. Each direct flight costs $75, $98, $120 or $150, depending on the length of the flight. If you change planes on a non-direct flight, it costs two coupons. You must pay for your trans-Atlantic flight, which means that frequent-flyer flights do not qualify. Cities served include Ankara, Berlin, Casablanca, Gibraltar, London, Lyon, Moscow, Paris, Prague and Stuttgart. You must reserve and pay for your pass seven days in advance of your first flight.

British Midland, ☎ (800) 788 0555
Discover Europe Airpass

This is one of the most flexible airpasses available. The minimum number of flights required is only one! The minor technicalities are that the Airpass must be purchased in conjunction with a transatlantic ticket (on any airline), prior to departing the US. Passengers must reside outside of Europe. Pricing is $109 each way for flights within the UK, as well as from the UK to Amsterdam, Brussels, Dublin or Paris. Flights to more distant spots, such as Copenhagen, Prague or Zurich, run $139 each way. You can start using your pass at any city in this network. There is no minimum or maximum number of flights, and tickets are fully changeable.

Iberia Airlines, ☎ (800) 772 4642
Visit Spain

This pass lets you fly in a circuit around Spain, without returning to any city more than once. You must start and stop the circuit in the same city. The minimum of four coupons costs $249, and each additional coupon costs $50. You must purchase your trans-Atlantic flight, rather than using frequent-flyer miles, in order to qualify. You need not fly to Europe on Iberia. A surcharge of $50 applies if you fly to the Canary Islands. All travel must be completed within 60 days. There is an additional $50 surcharge for travel between June 15th and September 30th.

Scandinavian Airlines (SAS), ☎ (800) 221 2350
Visit Scandinavia Pass

This pass covers flights anywhere SAS flies in Denmark, Norway and Sweden. The first two segments cost $80, the next two cost $70, and the last two cost $60. You can purchase a minimum of one and a maximum of six coupons. You must choose your destinations in advance. Dates can be changed at no charge, but changing destinations will cost you $50.

LATIN AMERICA

Aero Peru, ☎ (800) 777 7717
Visit South America

195

Aero Peru's pass is a package deal, which includes a round-trip flight from the United States to Lima. Prices increase during the high season, from July 1st to August 15th. From Miami you get a round-trip to Lima plus six South American flights for $999, or $1,184 in high season. From Los Angeles it's $1,396 or $1,580. All South American flights go through Lima, so you really get a flight to Lima plus the opportunity to visit three of the following countries: Argentina, Bolivia, Brazil, Chile, Colombia or Ecuador. The exception of the Lima rule is that the flight from Santiago to Buenos Aires is direct. Extra segments cost $100 each. All flights must be completed within 45 days.

Mexicana Airlines, ☎ (800) 531 7921
Discover Mexico

Prices are lower than regular excursion fares, but not as good as the lowest discounted fares. Prices are determined by the city pairs involved. International travel on Aeromexico or Mexicana is required. Travelers must purchase a minimum of three coupons, two of which can be international segments. Sample itinerary: San Francisco–Mexico City–Cancun–Mazatlan–Mexico City–San Francisco for $1,038. You must stay a minimum of two days, and a maximum of 45. Tickets become nonrefundable after commencement of travel.

NORTH AMERICA

AirBC, ☎ (800) 456 5717
AirPass

Regional airline AirBC offers California residents traveling in Western Canada passes for unlimited standby flights. AirBC flights from Portland and Seattle to Vancouver are also included. The price is $329 for one week's unlimited travel, or $439 for two weeks. The pass must be purchased in California. AirBC's territory covers British Columbia, Alberta, Saskatchewan and Manitoba.

American Airlines, ☎ (800) 433 7300
Visit USA Pass

This pass is sold only in conjunction with a transatlantic fare bought in a foreign country. Travelers can buy between 3 and 14 coupons. The price is $549 for a booklet of three coupons, and then $100 for each additional coupon. A 24-hour advance reservation is required for each flight. Travelers should purchase this pass when they buy their international ticket.

America West Airlines, ☎ (800) 235 9292
Visit USA

Tickets must be purchased before arrival in the United States, and are nonrefundable, non-endorsable, and valid only on America West. Reservations are permitted, as is flying standby. You must decide which cities you want to visit in advance, and confirm your first flight. The rest can be left open, but you are better off reserving all of your flights, and changing them later if necessary. There are actually two programs here: the System Program gives you a minimum of 4 flights (maximum of 12) within the continental U.S. for $319. Cities served include New York, Washington D.C., Orlando, Chicago, San Francisco and Los Angeles, among others. The Tri-State program starts at $139 for a minimum of 2 coupons, valid only in California, Nevada and Arizona. Add-on coupons to Mexico City and the Grand Canyon are available for enrollees in either program. The fine print reads "To be eligible for this program, applicants must reside at least 100 miles beyond any U.S. border in a country or commonwealth territory other than the 50 United States and the District of Columbia, and arrive via the scheduled services of any air carrier." Travelers originating in Asia or Australia should contact their local America West office, or the agent issuing the international tickets, in order to get the specific fare on these passes. Many longer flights connect through Phoenix or Las Vegas; if you must change planes there, it will cost you two coupons, so try to book direct flights.

Senior Pass: Seniors can buy a booklet of four coupons for $495, or eight coupons for $920. Each coupon is good for a one-way flight anywhere in the continental US that is covered by America West.

Continental Airlines, ☎ (800) 435 0040
Visit USA Fare

This pass, which must be purchased outside the US, allows you to buy between three and ten coupons for between $309 and $659. Dates may remain open but complete routing must be specified. Ticket must be issued in conjunction with an international ticket. Coupons expire after 60 days. Except at Denver, Houston and Newark, changing planes at a connecting airport counts as a stopover and requires an additional coupon. Reservations must be confirmed before commencement of each flight. This is the cheapest standard air pass in the USA, but it can be hard to find space on the most popular flights during peak season.

Senior Air Pass: A 4-coupon book costs $579, and covers 4 one-way or 2 round-trip flights. To confirm a flight, you must book at least 14 days in advance; otherwise, you fly standby. An 8-coupon book sells for $999. Continental also offers a $999 Freedom Passport, which lets seniors (those over age 62) take one one-way domestic coach flight per week for four months. Time and day of week restrictions apply, and a Sunday night stay is required.

Hawaiian Airlines, ☎ (800) 367 5320
Hawaiian Air Pass

Under this program, pass holders can take an unlimited number of flights anywhere in the state of Hawaii for the duration of the pass. All flights must be reserved in advance, even if only moments in advance from an airport telephone. Hawaiians can buy this pass if they do it in conjunction with a flight to and from the mainland. Prices are as follows: five days for $169, seven days for $189, ten days for $229, and fourteen days for $269. Hawaiian also offers an inter-island program, with coupons running about $38 each.

Kiwi International Airlines, ☎ (800) 538 5494
Kiwi Bonus Pack

The pack includes six coupons good for one-way flights between the Newark hub and Atlanta, Chicago and Orlando. Tickets are valid for one full year from date of first flight. The Bonus Pack costs $590, or $98 per segment.

Northwest Airlines (call your travel agent outside the USA)
See America Pass

Travelers must purchase this pass abroad, and in fact will find Northwest agents in the United States quite unwilling to divulge information on this program. Prices are lowest if you purchase the pass in conjunction with an international flight on Northwest. Also,

prices increase a bit for summer and holiday periods. You may buy
between three and ten coupons, which in low season will cost you a
total of $349 to $709. You must determine your routing in advance,
but you can leave the dates open. Passes expire 60 days after the first
coupon is used, or 120 days after arrival in the USA, whichever comes
first. Only two stopovers are permitted at any one point, and only two
round-trip transcontinental flights without enroute stopovers are permitted.

Trans World Airlines, ☎ (800) 221 2000
Youth Travel Pack
Senior Travel Pack

For travelers age 14-24 who are full-time students, TWA's Youth
Travel Pack can be a great deal. A coupon book of 4 one-way tickets
costs $498. Sundays from noon to 7pm are blacked out. Reservations
must be made between 14 and 21 days in advance, unless you are
willing to fly standby. Each coupon is good for any one-way domestic flight. TWA's Senior Travel Pack ($489 for 4 coupons) has similar
restrictions, but is for persons aged 62 or over only. The TWA senior
program is also the only one we know of that offers coupon books
for a non-senior to accompany a qualifying senior. A book of four
such companion coupons runs $648.

Low-Fare Airlines

Americans are always complaining about how high domestic airfares are. Far too often, I hear people say things like, "I could fly to Europe for less than they want to charge me for this domestic flight!" Good old Southwest Airlines has done a great job of making domestic flights cheap again. In fact, they have been so successful, they have spawned a whole new category: low-fare airlines. Their prices are often less than half of the lowest fares charged by the major airlines. In fact, when the low-fare airlines and the majors offer the same fare on the same route, we fly the low-fare airline. We know that when a low-fare carrier starts a new route, the major airlines usually match the lower fare for a few seats on each plane. If the upstarts leave a market, the fares go back up. So support the little guys.

As these upstarts are proving, charging a fair price is more important than having a big name. This is especially true when tickets are purchased by small companies and vacationers. The public seems most receptive to "no-frills" flights on short hops, which don't last long enough for anyone to start feeling too deprived. In fact, the traveling public has responded quite favorably to the new carriers. Significant increases in passenger traffic have been noted in most low-fare markets. Where people once drove, took the train, or simply did not make the trip, they are now taking advantage of the low fares and traveling by plane.

The following section gives you a rundown of the low-fare airline line-up.

Air 21
☎ (800) FLY AIR 21

Based in: Fresno, CA
First flight: 1995
Airline code: A7
Frequent-flyer club: None
Region served: West Coast, USA
Service to: Fresno, Las Vegas, Palm Springs, Redmond, San Francisco, Seattle

Air 21 flies all short routes, and uses a ticketless system. Some airlines limit the number of seats that are available at the lowest fare. Not Air 21; every seat on every plane is the same price, every day. Their slo-gan, "low fares, big planes," highlights the fact that they use full-size jets where other airlines would use turboprops. All fares are nonre-fundable and non-transferable, but dates or destinations can be changed for $21. The reservations line is open only from 6am to 9:30pm daily, PST.

Low-Fare Airlines

Air South
☎ (800) AIR SOUTH

Based in: Columbia, SC
First flight: 1994
Airline code: WV
Frequent-flyer club: One free round trip for every eight paid round trips
Region served: Southeastern USA
Service to: Atlanta, Columbia, Jacksonville, Miami, Myrtle Beach, Raleigh/Durham, Tallahassee, Tampa

Air South flies 737s (like Southwest) on short hauls. Their best fares require a 21-day advance purchase. They can be ticketed over on-line systems like SABRE, which is a real advantage over competitor ValuJet. Sample fare: Atlanta to Miami for $158 round trip.

AirTran Airways
☎ (800) 247 8726
Based in: Orlando
First flight: 1995
Airline code: FL
Frequent-flyer club: None
Region served: Eastern USA
Service to: Akron, Albany, Allentown, Buffalo, Cincinnati, Dallas, Dayton, Greensboro, Hartford, Kansas City, Knoxville, Nashville, Norfolk, Omaha, Orlando, Providence, Rochester, Salem (NC), San Antonio, Syracuse

Tickets are nonrefundable. A ticket change fee of $25 applies. Fares are sold on a capacity controlled basis, with the cheapest seats selling out first. The airline offers nonstop, Boeing 737 jet service. Sample fare: Akron to Orlando for $200 round trip.

American Trans Air

☎ (800) 225 2995

Based in: Indianapolis
First flight: 1973
Airline code: TZ
http://www.xmission.com/~aoi/fata.html
Frequent-flyer club: None
Region served: USA
Service to: Belfast, Boston, Cancun, Chicago, Dublin, Ft. Lauderdale, Honolulu, Indianapolis, Las Vegas, Los Angeles, Maui, Miami, Milwaukee, Nassau, New York (JFK), Orlando, Phoenix, Riga, Salt Lake City, San Francisco, Sarasota, Shannon, St. Petersburg, West Palm Beach

ATA runs charter planes, which it fills by selling seats directly to passengers as well as to tour operators. The charter operation gives ATA the flexibility to move into (and out of) markets quickly, taking advantage of trends before the majors can make adjustments. The airline was founded by a Latvian immigrant who started with a single plane. Their peak season runs from December through April, which leads to some particularly good deals in the summer months. One caveat: ATA's seats are as cramped as its prices are low. Sample fare: San Francisco to New York for $378 round trip.

British Midland

☎ (800) 788 0555

Based in: Derby, England
First flight: 1982
Airline code: BD
http://www.iflybritishmidland.com
Frequent-flyer club: In-house program tied to American AAdvantage, United Airlines Mileage Plus, and Virgin Atlantic Freeway
Region served: Europe
Service to: Amsterdam, Belfast, Bergen, Birmingham, Brussels, Copenhagen, Dublin, East Midlands, Edinburgh, Frankfurt, Glasgow, Guernsey, Jersey, Leeds Bradford, London, Malaga, Nice, Palma, Paris, Prague, Teesside, Zurich

British Midland is one of the first low-fare, short-haul airlines in Europe. They began competing on British Airways' home turf in 1979, and in 1986 became one of the first airlines to take advantage of airline deregulation in Europe. Their first flight to the continent, from London to Amsterdam, occurred in 1986. British Midland's Discover Europe Airpass is one of the most flexible airpasses available. The minimum number of flights required is only one! Flights within the UK or to nearby foreign cities run $109 each way, while flights to more distant spots, such as Copenhagen, Prague or Zurich, run $139 each way. See the Air Pass section (Chapter 17) for details.

Eastwind Airlines
☎ (800) 644 3592

Based in: Trenton NJ
First flight: 1995
Airline code: W9
http://pages.prodigy.com/X/S/A/XSNN68A/eastwind.htm or
http://www.prodworks.com/trenton/travel.htm
Region served: East Coast USA
Service to: Boston, Greensboro, Jacksonville, Orlando, Trenton, West Palm Beach

Uses all 737's. No advance purchase or weekend stayover required. Sample fare: Boston to Jacksonville, $260 round trip.

Frontier Airlines
☎ (800) 4321 FLY
Based in: Denver
First flight: 1995
Airline code: F9
http://www.cucruising.com/cu/frontier.html
Frequent-flyer club: Continental's OnePass or in-house program
Region served: USA-Southwest, Midwest, West
Service to: Albuquerque, Bismark, Chicago (Midway), El Paso, Fargo, Las Vegas, Los Angeles, Minneapolis/St. Paul, Omaha, Phoenix, Salt Lake City, San Diego, San Francisco, Seattle, St. Louis

Frontier's stated mission is to "bring low-fare service to Denver's most popular air travel markets." Flying a fleet of Boeing 737s, Frontier was formed to take advantage of the void created when Continental Airlines downsized its Denver hub. The airline's discount fares are up to 40 percent off the fares that existed in each market prior to Frontier's entry. Amenities include premium legroom and upscale snacks like bagels and cream cheese, oversize muffins, and heated servings of assorted nuts.

Horizon Air
☎ (800) 547 9308

Based in: Seattle
First flight: 1981
Airline code: AS
http://www.horizonair.com/
Frequent-flyer club: Alaska Airlines, TWA, Northwest, British Airways
Region served: North America–Pacific Northwest, British Columbia, Alberta
Service to: Bellingham, Billings, Boise, Bozeman, Butte, Calgary, Edmonton, Eugene, Eureka/Arcata, Great Falls, Helena, Idaho Falls, Jackson Hole, Kalispell, Klamath Falls, Lewiston, Medford, Missoula, Oakland, Portland, Redding, Redmond/Bend, Sacramento, San Jose, Seattle, Spokane, Sun Valley, Twin Falls, Vancouver, Victoria, Walla Walla, Wenatchee, Yakima

Horizon is owned by Alaska Airlines, but is operated separately. Ticketless reservations can be made through their "Instant Travel" program. Sample fare: service linking the high-tech computer centers of San Jose and Boise for $79.

KIWI International Air Lines Inc.
☎ (800) JET KIWI

Based in: Newark, NJ
First flight: 1992
Airline code: KP
Frequent-flyer club: In-house
Region served: Eastern USA
Service to: Atlanta, Bermuda, Chicago (Midway), Las Vegas, New York (Newark), Orlando, Tampa, West Palm Beach

Employee-owned Kiwi was started by former Pan Am and Eastern Airlines workers. Pilots put in $50,000 apiece, and other employees contributed $5,000 each. When Continental tried to crush the fledgling Kiwi with a fare war, its employee-owners agreed to a 50 percent pay cut for everyone except single parents. They used the savings to cut fares, and were able to beat back Continental's challenge. Their walk-up fares are 25 to 50 percent less than those charged by the major airlines on the same routes. In response, major corporations such as AT&T and RJR Nabisco have made Kiwi a preferred supplier. Kiwi hubs at Newark and Chicago Midway serve Atlanta, Puerto Rico, and various Florida sunspots. The airline has its own frequent-flyer program. Changes cost $25 and cancellations are $50. There are no advance-purchase or minimum-stay requirements. However, you cannot buy one-way tickets without paying a higher price, and you must book early to get the lowest-priced capacity-controlled seats. Food quality, service and legroom are far above average. Sample fare: Newark to West Palm Beach for $238 round trip.

Martinair Holland
☎ (800) MARTINAIR

Based in: Amsterdam
First flight: 1958
Airline code: MP
Frequent-flyer club: None
Region served: Worldwide
Service to: Amsterdam from: Denver, Edmonton, Los Angeles, Miami, New York (Newark), Orlando, San Francisco (Oakland), Seattle, Tampa, Toronto, Vancouver

Previously a charter airline, Martinair now offers scheduled service from all of its US gateways. In addition to its long-haul flights to Europe, Martinair offers short-haul flights from Amsterdam to Mediterranean destinations and to the Canary Islands. Martinair is one of the few airlines that lets you fly standby. Their one-way standby fares run $250-300 from the US to Amsterdam. Keep in mind that there is no standby program on the way back. Contact a consolidator in Europe when you are ready to come home.

Midway Airlines

☎ (800) 446 4392

Based in: Durham NC
First flight: 1993
Airline code: JI
Frequent-flyer club: American AAdvantage
Region served: Mostly Eastern USA
Service to: Boston, Cancun, Ft. Lauderdale, Hartford, Las Vegas, New York (Laguardia/Newark), Orlando, Philadelphia, Providence, Raleigh/Durham, Stewart/Newburg, Tampa, Washington DC, West Palm Beach

This Midway was started by new investors in 1993, and is independent of the previous Midway, which went bankrupt in 1991. The new Midway's routes run from Chicago to Dallas, Denver, New York LaGuardia, Philadelphia and Washington, D.C. Fares vary slightly depending on refundability, seven-day advance purchase, and Saturday night stay. Seating is better than average. Sample fare: New York to Chicago for $99 each way.

Midwest Express

☎ (800) 452 2022

Based in: Milwaukee
First flight: 1984
Airline code: YX
http://www.cwru.edu/Cleve/hopkins/midwest.html
Frequent-flyer club: In-house
Region served: USA
Service to: Appleton (WI), Atlanta, Boston, Cleveland, Columbus, Dallas, Denver, Ft. Lauderdale, Ft. Myers, Grand Rapids, Kansas City, Las Vegas, Los Angeles, Madison, New York, Newark, Omaha, San Diego, San Francisco, Tampa, Toronto, Washington DC

This company's angle might just catch on: they offer near-first-class service at coach prices. On DC-9s where most airlines would install five seats per row, Midwest Express has only four. They also use cloth napkins and offer free wine on all flights. Frequent-flyer miles can also be used on Air New Zealand, Scandinavian Airlines, and Virgin Atlantic. This company was born as the in-house airline for Kimberly-

Clark business travelers. Routes extend to both coasts from
Milwaukee, whose Mitchell Airport is becoming a popular alternative
to Chicago's O'Hare. The cheapest flights are nonrefundable, require
a Friday or Saturday night stay, and require a 14-day advance purchase. Sample fare: Milwaukee to Los Angeles round trip for $298.

Nations Air Express
☎ (800) 248 9538

Based in: Atlanta
First flight: 1995
Airline code: N5
Frequent-flyer club: None
Region served: Eastern USA
Service to: Atlanta, Boston, Fort Myers, Gulfport (MS), Orlando,
Philadelphia, Pittsburg, St. Petersburg, West Palm Beach

Nations Air is following the low-cost, low-fare, ticketless strategy.
Expect the cities served to change often as the airline continues to
grow.

Southwest Airlines
☎ (800) I FLY SWA

Based in: Dallas
First flight: 1971
Airline code: WN
http://www.iflyswa.com
Frequent-flyer club: Rapid Rewards
Region served: USA
Service to: Albuquerque, Amarillo, Austin, Baltimore/Washington,
Birmingham, Boise, Burbank, Chicago, Cleveland, Columbus,
Corpus Christi, Dallas, Detroit, El Paso, Ft. Lauderdale, Houston,
Indianapolis, Kansas City, Las Vegas, Little Rock, Los Angeles,
Louisville, Lubbock, Midland/Odessa, Nashville, New Orleans,
Oakland, Oklahoma City, Omaha, Ontario (CA), Orange County,
Phoenix, Portland, Reno, Rio Grande Valley (Harlingen), Sacramento,
Salt Lake City, San Antonio, San Diego, San Francisco, San Jose,
Seattle, Spokane, St. Louis, Tampa, Tulsa, Tucson

The pioneer in low-fare short flights, Southwest's strategy has been to lure passengers off the highways by making flying and driving competitive in price. During one fare war, Southwest was charging $19 each way from Cleveland to Baltimore, when the bus fare between the same cities was $44. They serve snacks instead of meals, and their frequent-flyer miles cannot be used on other carriers, but at these prices, no one is complaining. Also, they service planes and get them back in the air faster than anyone else in the business. Southwest recently took over Morris Air, which ran an incredibly similar operation in the Rocky Mountains region. *USA Today* has estimated that Southwest influences one-third of all domestic airfares. While charging less, Southwest also somehow manages to offer good, basic service. In fact, Southwest has won the "Triple Crown" every year from 1992 to present: they have had the best on-time percentage of all major US carriers, the best luggage handling, and the least complaints to the Department of Transportation. Reports indicate that Southwest plans to launch service at a small New England airport (perhaps Providence, RI) in the latter half of 1996. If the reports are accurate, this means that Southwest is expanding to the only area in the US they do not yet cover, and offering a convenient alternative to the congestion at Boston's Logan International Airport. Sample fare: San Francisco to Los Angeles for $49 each way.

Spirit Airlines
☎ (800) 772 7117

Based in: Detroit
First flight: 1992
Airline code: NK
Frequent-flyer club: None
Region served: Eastern USA
Service to: Atlantic City, Boston, Detroit, Ft. Lauderdale, Ft. Myers, Myrtle Beach, Orlando, Philadelphia, Tampa

Spirit's cheapest fares are capacity-controlled (so call early) and require round-trip purchase, but have no minimum stay. Spirit was previously a charter-only airline, and moved into scheduled flights in May 1992. They usually have one round-trip flight per day for each pair of cities. Sample fare: Detroit to Orlando for $139 round trip.

Tower Air

☎ (800) 34 TOWER, (718) 553 8500

Based at JFK Airport, NY
First flight: 1984
Airline code: FF
Frequent-flyer club: None
Region served: USA, Middle East, Asia, Europe
Service to: Amsterdam, Bombay, Los Angeles, Miami, New York,
Paris, Rio de Janeiro, San Francisco, San Juan, Sao Paulo, Tel Aviv

Tower is unique among the low-fare carriers in that it focuses on longer flights, competing directly with the profit centers of the major airlines. Business class costs only $75 more than coach on most domestic flights. There are no restrictions, and no meals. Seats are much more comfortable than average. Sample fare: New York to San Francisco for $318 round trip.

ValuJet

☎ (800) 825 8538

Based in: Atlanta
First flight: 1993
Airline code: J7
http://www.valujet.com
Frequent-flyer club: None
Region served: USA–Northeast, Southeast, Midwest
Service to: Atlanta, Boston, Charlotte, Chicago, Columbus, Dallas, Detroit, Ft. Lauderdale, Ft. Myers, Hartford, Kansas City, Louisville, Memphis, Miami, Mobile, Nashville, New Orleans, Norfolk, New York, Orlando, Philadelphia, Pittsburg, Raleigh/Durham, Savannah, Tampa, Washington DC, West Palm Beach

ValuJet promotes an informal, no-frills image. Most of its flights are in the Southeast, but range from Philadelphia and Chicago to Miami and Dallas. Their fare structure has three levels: the cheapest is for 21-day advance purchases, next best is 7-day advance, and still good is the walk-up fare. Tickets are nonrefundable, but no Saturday night stays or round-trip purchases are required. Paper tickets as such are never even issued. ValuJet uses an advanced electronic booking system, and gives each passenger a confirmation number instead of a ticket. Starting in mid-1996, Valujet brings low-fare service to the New York area, with five flights a day from Atlanta to LaGuardia. From Atlanta the airline offers connections to over two dozen cities east of the Mississipi. Sample fare: Atlanta to Jacksonville one way for $39 with a 21-day advance purchase, or $89 as a walk-up fare.

Vanguard Airlines
☎ (800) 826 4827

Based in: Kansas City
First flight: 1995
Airline code: NJ
http://www.cucruising.com/cu/vanguard.html
Frequent-flyer club: None
Region served: Western and Midwestern USA
Service to: Chicago (Midway), Dallas, Denver, Des Moines, Kansas City, Minneapolis, Salt Lake City, San Francisco, Wichita

From a Vanguard ad: "Now, if for some reason you can't use a seat you booked on Vanguard on the day you planned to travel, you have up to 90 days from the flight date to fly with us. If you don't rebook within 90 days, it's like a ballgame ticket—you use it or lose it. There's a $25 charge for changing your mind (same day changes are no charge). Our best fares require 14-day advance purchase. Seats are limited and may not be available on every flight." In Kansas City, Vanguard has found an underserved market that seems to appreciate the low-fare concept. Sample fare: San Francisco to Chicago for $252 round trip.

Western Pacific
☎ (800) 930 3030

Based in: Colorado Springs (near Denver)
First flight: 1995
Airline code: W7
http://www.cucruising.com/cu/wpair.html
Frequent-flyer club: None
Region served: USA
Service to: Atlanta, Chicago Midway, Dallas, Houston, Indianapolis, Kansas City, Las Vegas, Los Angeles, Nashville, New York (Newark),

Oklahoma City, Phoenix, Portland, San Antonio, San Diego, San Francisco, San Jose, Seattle, Tulsa, Washington DC, Wichita

WestPac, as the company has nicknamed itself, flies all Boeing 737 aircraft. Colorado Springs is its hub, so all flights involve a stop there. They use a "ticketless" reservation system, and give you a personal identification number to use at check-in. WestPac's strategy includes a medium-haul route structure based on low fares and no meals, no frills and casually dressed employees. Their innovative "air logo" program turns their 737s into flying billboards. They also pay airline fees of only $4.70 per passenger at Colorado Springs, as compared to about $18 per passenger at the new Denver International Airport. Their best fares require a 21-day advance purchase. Fares are better off peak, which means Tuesday, Wednesday or Saturday, plus some mornings. Sample fare: San Francisco to Chicago for $264 round trip.

Who Says Standby Flights are Dead?

CHAPTER 18

Years ago, you could walk up to the airport ticket counter minutes before departure, and if empty seats remained, you could fly at the very low "standby" price. Then someone from the airlines realized that they could probably make more money by forcing last-minute travelers to pay a premium, and the standby flight nearly disappeared.

I say nearly, because standby fares can still be found, if you know where to look. The airlines no longer sell standbys, but certain discount travel agencies still do. The logic is this: you buy a standby ticket for a certain date, at a very good price. The airline continues to try to sell your seat. If someone comes to the airport 15 minutes before departure, he will have to pay the airline's premium, but he will get your seat. If they still have empty seats at departure time, then you are allowed to board, and the airline has gained some revenue.

It is a win-win situation, as long as you have a backup plan in case you don't get onto the plane. If the next flight is in a few hours, this is probably a good deal. If you live near the airport, and it won't be a huge inconvenience for you to return to the airport another day, it is still a good deal. But if it will cause you great emotional pain to miss the flight, pay the extra money for a confirmed seat.

Another time to use standby fares is when all of the discounted seats on a flight are sold out. Chances are good that some of the higher-priced seats will remain open, and standby passengers will be allowed to fill those seats. But by their very nature, standby flights are not a sure thing. If your plans are flexible enough, here are some discount agencies that deal in standby fares.

Air-Tech Ltd. (New York)
☎ (212) 219 7000

Air-Tech specializes in region-to-region standby travel. Most of their flights connect Baltimore, Boston, Cleveland, Chicago, Los Angeles, Miami, New York and San Francisco with major Western European cities, and with Mexico and the Caribbean. You purchase a Flightpass voucher from them, which you exchange for a boarding pass at the airport, if space is available on the flight. You must be flexible in both destination and date of travel. They ask you to list three major cities that would be acceptable as destinations, and to provide a "travel window" of acceptable departure dates. A few days before your window starts, call to find out which flights offer the best odds. You may end up flying to Amsterdam on Wednesday, instead of to London on Tuesday. If this kind of system works for you, give them a call. Summer one-way prices to Western Europe are $169 from the East Coast, or $269 from California. (Air-Tech also offers occasional courier flights, mostly to Asia. Call them for details.)

Discount Travel International
☎ (800) FLY 4 DTI

DTI is constantly foraging for new bargains, so you should call them to get the latest information. In general, they book standby seats on the low-fare airlines for flights within the USA, and also book flights on some of the most popular international routes. Flights typically depart from most major U.S. airports. DTI also sells discounted confirmed seats on most of the same flights. Sample fare: one-way New York to Miami for $125 standby, or $149 confirmed.

Now Voyager (New York)
☎ (718) 656 5000

Now Voyager offers a wide variety of coast-to-coast standbys, as well as occasional international bargains. Call and listen to their recording for details.

Get "Bumped" and Fly Free Next Time

Across the country, thousands of air travelers are voluntarily giving up their confirmed seats on oversold flights. Why, you ask? Because the airlines make it worthwhile.

Airlines regularly sell more tickets than there are seats on the plane. The purpose of this "overbooking" is to make up for the estimated 10 percent of customers who fail to show up for a scheduled flight.

When flights are overbooked, airlines would rather leave volunteers behind than force people to miss flights. When the airlines need to "bump" someone from a flight, they offer incentives to encourage people to volunteer.

If you get bumped, you get priority for the next available flight. Also, you usually get a free round-trip flight to be used at a later date. Often you get free meals and a free hotel room, too.

If your schedule allows it, there are ways of increasing your chance of being bumped and getting a free flight.

Reserve a seat on a popular flight. Find out which flights are busiest. To avoid suspicion you might say, "I have a friend who is also interested in that flight. How does it look for her?" If you must arrive somewhere on a specific day, make sure there is a flight with available seating following the one from which you hope to be bumped. This way, if you are lucky enough to get bumped, you can still arrive that same day.

If you are completely flexible about when you fly, put yourself on the waiting list of several busy flights. That way, if you do get a confirmed seat on one, you'll know it's full, and you will have vastly improved your chance of getting bumped.

Travel when the airlines are the busiest. Try Thanksgiving, Christmas, and other holidays. Monday, Friday and Sunday are the busiest days of the week. Early-morning departures and early-evening arrivals are the most popular flights.

Arrive at the airport early. When you check in, ask if the flight is full. Volunteer to get bumped as soon as you have a boarding pass, before the airline announces that the flight is overbooked. Get your name near the top of the waiting list; if you wait until just before takeoff, there will be a teeming horde of volunteers ahead of you.

Sometimes the airlines engage in "bidding for bumpees." At first they offer something small, such as a $50 coupon towards a future flight. If enough people voluntarily give up their seats for $50 each, the airlines save a lot of money. If they still need to vacate some seats, they may up the offer to a one-way transcontinental flight. Be aware of their little bidding game, and hang in there as long as it seems advantageous. I look for a free round-trip ticket any time I save an airline's reputation for service by giving up my seat.

Courier Adventures

CHAPTER *20*

Courier travel is so easy—it amazes me that more people do not take advantage of it. Your duties are simple and not burdensome, yet your airfare is half that of other passengers. And if you are a seasoned traveler, you probably already pack light and bring only carry-ons.

To illustrate how easy it is to fly as a courier, consider the following stories:

"Joe Can't Make It; Welcome to Japan"

Steve Rubenstein is a columnist for the San Francisco Chronicle. *In this two-part column, Steve recounts his Singapore courier experience, which was booked at the last minute, and included a stopover in Japan.*

They sent me to the other side of the world last week. I was to meet the man in the black windbreaker.

Someone had to do it. Someone trustworthy. They sent me anyway.

The mission was to go to Tokyo and Singapore, and hand a slip of paper to a man in a black windbreaker. This is the job of the international air courier. A courier flies around the world on a moment's notice. On the other side of the world, the courier hands over his baggage claim check.

"Think you can do that?" said the courier dispatcher.

Yes. I do. I went to college.

"Good," she said. "Then we're sending you to Tokyo and Singapore. You leave the day after tomorrow."

Couriers are the latest fuzzy gray area in international travel. Overnight mail companies recruit couriers to carry sacks of express mail as baggage, because passenger baggage clears customs faster than unaccompanied cargo. The actual courier, who pays nothing or next to nothing to fly around the world, is something of a technicality. The courier carries nothing himself, and never touches the mail sacks.

"You just sit on the plane," she said.

The courier nodded. Being a newspaperman in his other life, he knows how to sit around, doing nothing.

Before departure at the airport came the final briefing from the head courier.

"When you get to Tokyo, you are to meet a man in a black windbreaker. His name is Joe. He'll be at the No. 1 customs counter. Give him this claim check."

The sack of express mail had already been checked onto the plane. What was inside the sack? the courier asked.

"You don't need to know." said the head courier. "Contracts, documents, boring stuff. A lot of paperwork."

Stick to the basics, he said. Fly around the world, meet Joe. Give him the scrap of paper.

The courier got on the plane. A flight attendant traipsed over and handed him a hot washcloth. Shortly after takeoff, the courier got another one. Singapore Airlines is big on hot washcloths. This was a seven-washcloth flight.

This was Tokyo. Outside was a city of 18 million people. With any luck, one of them would be wearing a black windbreaker. There he was, inside the customs hall, at Counter No. 1.

"Joe?"

It wasn't Joe. Joe couldn't make it, he said. The courier had flown around the world to meet Joe, and Joe wasn't there.

The guy in the windbreaker said his name was Endo. The courier handed him the claim check.

"It's OK," he said. "I don't need the claim check. You can keep it."

Wait a minute, windbreaker man. The courier flew halfway around the world to give you a claim check, and now you don't want it?

"They know me here," he said. "I already picked up the sack. Welcome to Japan."

© *San Francisco Chronicle*. Reprinted by permission.

The Only Danger Was in My Head: A Woman's View on Flying Courier

"I understand you're looking for someone to take a last-minute courier flight to Bangkok?"

"Yes," said the man on the other end. "We need someone to cover a flight next week."

"Perfect." For days, I had been shopping around for a one-way flight out of Hong Kong to no avail. Even the cheapest flights cost more than a round-trip ticket. Finally, a travel agent in the Chung King Mansions pointed me towards this small company, which sometimes needed last-minute couriers. The courier man and I agreed to meet so I could sign the necessary paperwork and pay the company a token sum.

The day of my meeting I put on my best freshly pressed skirt and blouse, with stockings and sandals. I'm a middle-aged female, and fretted that perhaps I was too old for this courier business. I was nervous. I wanted to be sure I looked trustworthy, and generally make a good impression.

I followed the man's directions to a messy, crowded, warehouse-like space in Kowloon. There was no office per se, but only a cluster of desks surrounded by filing cabinets, overflowing wastebaskets and clutter.

I was glad I had already flown courier once before. That was in the United States some ten years ago, back when you could still get domestic courier flights. My son was going to school in New York at the time, and I was living in Los Angeles. A friend offered me a free round-trip flight to New York for the weekend. I accepted, even though I was afraid I might be doing something a bit shady. Back in 1982, I had never heard of flying as a courier. I pictured myself sitting with a valuable package balanced on my knees all the way across the country. "You're going to wind up in jail for drug smuggling," my brother warned. Why else would a company want a person to take something across the country for them? At the luggage carousel in New York, I turned in my claims check. My worries quickly abated when my cargo turned out to be several large canvas sacks with "Chase Manhattan Bank" stencilled across them.

This time around, the Hong Kong courier representative informed me that my job would be even easier. "You won't even touch any packages here or in Bangkok. Give the claim checks to the man you will meet at the airport. He will take you wherever you want to stay in Bangkok." Because my flight would arrive after midnight, I was relieved that arrangements had been made for my ground transportation.

In the Bangkok customs clearance area, there was a special aisle just for couriers. Clearing customs was quicker and easier for me than for a regular tourist. Apparently, a special arrangement allows the courier company representative into this customs area to meet me. He arrived wearing a gaudy floral print shirt that looked Hawaiian.

The tiny car was really full. The highway was nearly empty. From Hong Kong, I phoned ahead to the family-run guest house where I usually stay in Bangkok. The family agreed to leave a gate key on top of the wall for me, in case I arrived late. The driver wove his way through the streets of Bangkok, until we finally arrived at the guest house's alleyway—one so narrow that only pedestrians can pass. I had arrived at my destination, and the gate wasn't even locked. I thanked my driver, and glanced in to find travelers still lounging in the common room. I should have been as relaxed as they. . . as it turned out, the only danger in flying as a courier was in my own head.

I entered the guest house compound and took off my shoes. I smiled to myself. I was back in exciting old Siam.

Lorraine Diamond is a Los Angeles-based philosopher, lab technician and aspiring writer. You have just read the first of what promises to be many published pieces by this talented storyteller.

Packing Light

To some it may seem to go against the grain of capitalist society, but when traveling, LESS IS MORE! The less gear you schlep around, the happier you will be.

Those taking courier flights are usually compelled to pack light. But all of us would do well to travel as light as couriers do. Buy a good backpack, and make sure it is small enough to fit on the plane. Ideally, the bag should have multiple compartments, and should convert from a backpack to a suitcase at the pull of a zipper. [A good example is the Maximum Legal Carry-On, by Patagonia, ☎ (800) 336 9090.]

What to pack? Everyone has slightly different needs, but the typical vacation traveler rarely will need more than the following for a two-week trip:

- **1** lightweight jacket
- **1** rain poncho
- **1** sweater or sweatshirt
- **3** shirts or blouses
- **1-2** pairs of pants or skirts
- **1-2** pairs of shorts
- **3** pairs of socks
- **4** changes of underwear
- **1** bathing suit
- **1** hat
- **1** pair of decent walking shoes
- **1** pair of beach/shower sandals
- **1** fairly nice outfit
- Toiletries
- Medicine
- Contraceptives
- Sunglasses
- The smallest towel you can stand
- Camera and film
- Pen light
- Multi-function knife
- Address book
- Travel alarm clock

Plastic bags for dirty laundry, etc.

Small day pack

Small, durable water bottle

Luggage locks

Maps and guidebooks

Pictures and postcards of home to show new friends

Documents, tickets, money, and a money belt to hold it all

Start with enough toiletries for only two weeks. Buy or borrow more as you go along. Bring a tube of liquid laundry detergent, and plan to wash a few items in your hotel sink every couple of days. Keep in mind that dark colors hide the dirt. Bring clothes that fit one or two color schemes, so you can wear anything with anything else. Avoid clothes that wrinkle easily. If you will be hostelling, bring a hostel sleep sack instead of renting one each night.

Traveling businesspeople can usually get away with one dark suit, an extra pair of pants/skirt, three shirts/blouses, and several ties/scarves (assuming frequent visits to the dry cleaners). The key is to foster the appearance of variety for the people you meet, not for yourself. If you are on a solo business trip and you will be seeing different clients each day, they'll never know what you wore yesterday.

Zip up your pack, put it on, and step outside. If you can't easily walk ten blocks with it on, go back and unpack some of those things you thought you "might" need. If you really need them, you can buy them there. Remember, there is a reason that experienced travelers pack light. They know they will be happier and more mobile than if they didn't.

Glossary of Terms

APEX / Acronym for "Advance Purchase Excursion" fare, which is typically the cheapest and most restricted fare you can buy directly from the airlines.

Around-the-world fares / A special class of consolidator ticket which usually involves using multiple airlines and stopovers to cheaply circumnavigate the globe, stopping to visit a number of predetermined cities.

Bucket shop / Consolidators who sell tickets directly to the public.

Carry-on baggage / The allotment of luggage you are allowed to bring on board the plane with you. On domestic U.S. flights, you can usually carry aboard one bag weighing less than 20 kilograms (44 pounds), and one bag small enough to fit under your seat. International flights may restrict you to a single carry-on bag. A carry-on limit of five kilograms could legally be enforced, but in reality this rarely happens on major international airlines. Often, those flying as couriers are allowed to bring only carry-on luggage.

Charter flights / The "Brand X" of the airline industry. Their distinct legal status makes it easy for them to alter routes as the seasons change. They run discounted flights to the most popular destinations at each time of year, often from major cities to sun or ski vacation spots.

Checked baggage / Luggage which is stored in the hold of the plane. On international flights, the limit is usually 20 kilograms (44 pounds). In the USA, the limit on domestic flights is two bags weighing a total of no more than 85 kilograms (140 pounds). Couriers typically must give up their checked baggage allotment in exchange for a discounted airfare.

Circle-Pacific fares / A special class of consolidator ticket which typically involves using multiple airlines and stopovers to fly around the Pacific Rim cheaply, stopping to visit a number of predetermined cities.

Consolidator / The "factory outlet stores" of the airline industry. These agents buy excess seats from the airlines, and sell them at a steep discount. *See also* Bucket shop, Wholesaler.

Courier flight / A little-known mode of air travel in which passengers trade their checked baggage allotment to an international shipping company in exchange for a steeply discounted airfare on a major airline.

Ethnic specialty agency / Small, local bucket shops, usually run by and catering to members of a particular ethnic group.

Exporting tickets / The practice of selling air tickets by mail to third countries to take advantage of particularly low airfares in some world markets. Most agents that can export tickets are in San Francisco and London. This practice is frowned upon by the airlines, but (depending on the agent's agreement with the airline) not against any law.

High season / The time of year when passenger demand (and therefore airfares) are highest. Varies depending on the destination. Typically July and August in Europe and North America, January and February in Australia, and around Christmas in most of the Western world.

IATA / The International Air Transport Association, a cartel of international airlines that attempts to regulate the price of air travel.

Local currency strategy / A discount airfare trick that works when, by exchanging money to a foreign currency and purchasing the ticket in that currency, the ticket is cheaper than buying the ticket in the currency of origin.

Low season / The time of year when few people seek to travel to a particular destination. Airline tickets are cheapest at this time.

One-way ticket / A ticket good only for travel from Point A to Point B. Known as a "single ticket" in the UK and Australia.

Onward ticket / A ticket valid for travel from Point A to Point B, and on to Point C. Often necessary at customs at Point B as proof that you don't plan to stay illegally in their country.

Open-jaw ticket / A ticket which lets you fly into one city, spend your vacation traveling by land, and return home from another city. For example, you might fly from the USA to London, travel by rail through Europe, and finally catch a flight in Athens to return to the USA.

Return ticket / A ticket valid for travel from Point A to Point B then returning back to Point A. Often necessary at customs at Point B, as proof that you don't plan to stay illegally in their country. Same as a round-trip ticket.

Round-trip ticket / *See* Return ticket.

Scheduled flight / The legal status of flights on most major airlines. Provides more protection to the passenger in case of a cancelled or delayed flight.

Shoulder season / The period between high and low season, during which demand for air travel (and therefore the cost of air travel) is moderate. Often the most cost-effective and least tourist-ridden time to travel.

Space-available fare / The modern equivalent of the old "standby fare." Passengers must purchase a space-available ticket at a special agency before arriving at the airport. Ten minutes before the flight, the ticket can be traded for a boarding pass if there are still empty seats on the plane.

Standby fare / Once the very cheap fare sold by airlines at the gate 10 minutes before departure. Now nearly nonexistent. Last-minute tickets purchased from the airline at the gate are among the most expensive fares available.

Sufficient funds / An arbitrary amount of money, possession of which you may need to demonstrate to customs officials as proof that you can support yourself while in their country. A credit card will often suffice.

Wholesaler / Consolidators who sell tickets only to retail travel agents.

Travel Resources

In preparing to research this book we consulted innumerable travel guides. We found the following guides particularly useful. If you plan to stay in a hub city for more than a few days, or to visit the surrounding area, these guidebooks and serials are among the best available.

The Berkeley Guides give some long overdue competition to *Let's Go* in the battle for the student market. The main difference between the two is the Berkeley trend towards covering more outdoor activities, and more ways to get involved, rather than just coming to watch.

Europe Through The Back Door takes you off the well-worn tourist track, and shows you the kinds of places that the locals patronize. Author Rick Steves tracks down family-run inns and restaurants that stay in business by offering good value to return customers rather than gouging tourists. Get Rick's free newsletter by calling ☎ (206) 771 8303, or e-mail ricksteves@aol.com.

The Hostel Handbook for the USA and Canada is the most efficient and cost-effective travel guidebook we have ever used. In a quick and to-the-point manner, it provides contact information and prices for almost every hostel in North America. The information is extremely fresh, being updated every spring for the current year's edition. Available at independent hostels, or by sending a check or money order for $3 (payable to Jim Williams) to 722 Saint Nicholas Avenue, New York, NY 10031, USA. For more information, call ☎ (212) 926 7030 or e-mail infohostel@aol.com.

Let's Go is the classic Europe handbook, and has been the bible for a generation of student travelers. Over the years they have added in-depth regional and country guides to most of Europe and North America.

Let's Party! guides help you find the best entertainment options available. At 5pm in most countries the museums close. But at about the same time, hundreds of other interesting locales are just opening. *Let's Party! Europe* shows you the best cafés, dance clubs, Irish pubs, and late-night food spots in 37 cities across the Continent. *Let's Party! San Francisco,* the second book in the series (co-authored by

Michael Wm. McColl), takes you neighborhood by neighborhood to see the mainstream and the obscure. If you like to meet the locals when you travel, these guidebooks will show you where they hang out. Look for more *Let's Party!* guides to US cities in 1996-97.

Lonely Planet guides cover most of the world, with a focus on off-the-beaten-track destinations. In fact, if you can get there only by backpacking in, this is the only guidebook likely to list it. Their *On a Shoestring* series covers large geographic areas from an ultra-budget perspective, while the *Travel Survival Kits* focus on smaller regions with a greater depth of coverage and wider price range.

Moon Handbooks do a great job of presenting historic and cultural background in a way that is relevant to the here-and-now of the independent traveler. Their practical information on accommodations and sights is highly reliable. We like their map-laden Southeast Asia volume, and look forward to trying out their broad series of guides to the rest of Asia, the Pacific, and North America. To subscribe to their free newsletter, *Travel Matters,* call ☎ (800) 345 5473.

The Native's Guide to New York City covers goings-on in the Big Apple like only a local could. Natives don't need accommodations, so you won't find them reviewed here. But if you are looking for a thousand things to do while in Manhattan (many of them free), author Richard Laermer's book is the one to get.

The Packing Book, by Judith Gilford, will teach you everything you need to know to travel light without looking wrinkled. By packing items that can be worn with several other packed items to create multiple outfits, and by knowing how to pack them properly, anyone can learn to travel out of a single carry-on bag. This book is particularly important for those traveling as couriers, but is useful for anyone who still isn't traveling as light as they would like. And for those who insist on bringing the kitchen sink, Judith now includes a section on how to pack checked luggage.

The Rough Guides dig deeper than most travel books to uncover things that only the hippest locals would know about. Their San Francisco book, for example, is utterly flawless. Every underground club and offbeat activity has been tracked down and accurately described. The down-to-earth and irreverent tone is sure to be appreciated by the independent budget traveler.

Salk International's Air Transport Guide gives you up-to-date transit information on over 400 airports around the world. Need to know how to get into downtown Bangkok after midnight, or how much to pay for a cab from Moscow Airport? It's all in here. If it saves you from just one luggage-laden wrong turn, the $8 you invested in this annual guidebook will have been more than worth it. To order, call ☎ (800) 828 CITY, or fax 415/ 433 3337.

Travelers' Tales (O'Reilly and Associates) is a new series which collects the firsthand experiences of some of the world's best travel writers. You won't find hotel and restaurant reviews, but short of living there yourself, there is no better way to get a feel for a country. Current guides cover Thailand, India and Mexico, with more in the works.

World Stompers is the compiled travel wisdom gleaned from author Brad Olsen's three-year, ultra-budget trip around the world. Sure, in a few years on the road, you could learn many of these travel secrets yourself. But that's what we call "learning the hard way." By reading this book before your trip, you will avoid a variety of travel scams and pitfalls, and be in a position to travel for as long as you want. Brad's tips and job-finding strategies are simply invaluable. This book is destined to become the backpacker's bible of the 1990s. If your favorite bookstore doesn't carry it yet, tell them to get with it! To order, they (or you) can call ☎ (415) 552 3628.

NEWSLETTERS AND MAGAZINES

Big World promotes cheap down-to-earth travel. Budget travel tips are crammed into each bimonthly issue. A regular column titled "The Virtual Traveler" points you toward the high-quality travel resources on the internet. Inspiring destination articles make you want to tell off your boss and hit the road. To subscribe, send $10 US / $15 Canada or Mexico / $20 overseas to Big World, Box 21, Coraopolis, PA 15108. For information, e-mail bigworld@aol.com.

Escape is the magazine for adventurous travelers who can now afford to travel comfortably, but who would still rather participate than watch when traveling. Incredible photography graces the pages of this substantial monthly. Practical tips cover outdoor activities such as river rafting and mountain biking. Featured offbeat destinations in one issue included Uzbekistan, Patagonia and Xishhuangbanna. To subscribe, send $18 ($25 Canada / $30 overseas) to Escape, Box 462255, Escondido, CA 92046. Or call ☎ (800) 738 5571.

The International Association of Air Travel Couriers has claimed the technological high ground in the courier newsletter field. They offer members two different bimonthly publications. Odd months, *The Air Courier Bulletin* provides updated courier information from most major U.S. cities as well as many foreign points. Even months, *The Shoestring Traveler* is full of personal travel accounts from the editors and members. Nifty high-tech features include a 24-hour fax-on-demand information retrieval system and a 24-hour computer bulletin board. These systems are great for those who need up-to-the-minute courier flight availability information, including hard-to-find last-minute mega-bargains. Via the bulletin board (now also accessible via internet, but by members only), you can also download articles from past issues, and trade thoughts with other association members. The IAATC's information is so up-to-date and extensive, we use it ourselves for many of the courier fares listed in this book. Subscriptions cost $42 a year. Write to PO Box 1349, Lake Worth, FL 33460, USA for an information packet or call ☎ (407) 582 8320.

Journeywoman offers a brash, unapologetically female take on travel. This quarterly magazine is full of practical, money-saving tips that men would find useful, too. But the primary message is that women should boldly venture forth to see the world for themselves. Solid first-hand accounts are enjoyable for armchair travelers as well; my favorite recent feature covered "Mexico's Red-Hot Mamas." ("In macho Mexico, the extraordinary Zapotec Indian women of Juchitan dominate their men, celebrating fatness and fertility. . . .") To subscribe, send US$24.07 to JW, 50 Prince Arthur Avenue, Suite 1703, Toronto, CANADA M5R 1B5. Or e-mail jwoman@web.net.

The South American Explorers Club is a loose confederation of academics and travelers who share a mutual interest in Latin America. This nonprofit organization publishes a quarterly newsletter full of stories and tips about the region. They also help bring people of similar interests together, either through their newsletter or through staffed clubhouses in Quito, Lima, and at the headquarters in Ithaca, NY. The clubs are meeting places for members, sources of current information, and can become a base camp for explorations of the region. For information, write the club at 126 Indian Creek Road,

region. For information, write the club at 126 Indian Creek Road, Ithaca, NY 14850. Telephone ☎ (607) 277 0488, or e-mail explorer@samexplo.org.

This next item is a way for travelers on domestic flights within the USA to get the same discounts that the big corporations and conventions get. **The Travel Confidential Society** offers a monthly newsletter outlining all of the airfare, hotel, and car rental discounts available to convention-goers nationwide. You don't necessarily have to attend the convention to get the discount airfare. The newsletter provides the code numbers you need to obtain these "confidential" group rates. Annual dues are $95, which may be deductible for businesspeople. The listings are extensive, and there is a six-month money-back guarantee. For more information on this impressive resource, call ☎ (800) 992 8972.

Travel Unlimited is the classic courier newsletter. Editor Steve Lantos' periodical has been instilling wanderlust in travelers since 1987. In addition to a monthly update of courier options, Travel Unlimited covers the latest trends in general low-budget travel. Subscriptions run $25 a year. For information and a free sample newsletter, write to PO Box 1058A, Allston, MA 02134, USA.

E-mail Travel Bargain Alert Service: For $29 a month, you can have the TravelGram VIP Bulletin delivered to your door (well, your e-mail account) on a daily basis. The recent trend in airfare discounting has been for the airlines to run underpublicized, super-short "sales," some of which last only 24 hours. TravelGram's research staff works full-time to track down these and other travel bargains. If a particular bargain can't wait until the next day, they send out a special alert via e-mail. Coverage includes hotels, car rentals, tours and other topics in addition to the airfare deals. Some of the bargains are published for free on the TravelGram web page, but to find out about everything, you will have to subscribe. To do so, send a check or money order for US$24 (drawn on a US bank) and your e-mail address to John Hart, 420 North Nellis Blvd., Bldg. A3, Suite 168, Las Vegas, NV 89110 USA. The free web page, in case you want to take a look at things first, is at http:www.travelgram.com/.

Trip is the magazine for those who travel with youthful vigor and occasional reckless abandon. This quarterly focuses on "exciting, affordable and doable adventures, ranging from rock climbing in Idyllwild and teaching in Milan to surfing in Baja and trekking through the Himalayas." The glossy, professional design is bold and fresh, as is the content. To subscribe, send $5 – yes, only $5 – (well, $12 if outside the US) to TRIP, 9 Latimer Road, Santa Monica, CA 90402. For information, e-mail triptravel@aol.com.

INDEX

234

EXPLORE THE EAST COAST WITH HOSTELLING INTERNATIONAL

New York

Miami Beach

Washington, DC

Boston

With Hostelling International you can visit some of America's exciting East Coast cities for a budget price. They're priced to fit a student's budget and are great places to meet people from all over the world. You can stay at a landmark building on the trendy Upper West Side of Manhattan, a highrise in the heart of the Nation's Capital, a historic masterpiece in Miami's Art Deco District, just two blocks from the ocean, or a handsomely refurbished turn-of-the-century guest house in the center of Boston, the Hub of New England. For reservations call:

New York City .... (212) 932-2300
Washington, DC .... (202) 737-2333
Miami Beach .... (305) 534-2988
Boston .... (617) 536-9455

HOSTELLING INTERNATIONAL
The new seal of approval of the International Youth Hostel Federation.

HOSTELLING INTERNATIONAL®

THE SHOESTRING
TRAVELER

The budget travel newsletter produced and published by members of the *International Association of Air Travel Couriers,* since 1989 the only travel group to stay in daily contact with air courier companies in the USA, Canada & the United Kingdom.

Also Available Online

- - -

See our Web Page at http://www.courier.org Or call our BBS direct at (561) 582-0425 and browse back issues online.

To obtain a <u>free</u> sample copy of *The Shoestring Traveler,* send your request in writing to: The Shoestring Traveler, c/o IAATC, PO Box 1349, Lake Worth, FL 33460.

-- Please mention *The Worldwide Guide to Cheap Airfares* --

How to Order More Books

The Worldwide Guide to Cheap Airfares makes a great gift for budget travelers. There are lots of ways you can order additional copies. First, check at your local bookstore. If they don't have it, you can order by telephone with a credit card. Call 24 hours a day, 365 days a year at ☎ (800) 78 BOOKS. [From outside the USA, call ☎ (415) 552 3600.] You can also complete the order form and fax your order to 415/ 552 1978. Or enclose a check or money order (in U.S. dollars) along with the form and mail it to the address below. Make checks payable to Insider Publications. Each copy costs $14.95 plus shipping ($2.50 for the first book, $1.00 for each additional book), and tax if necessary ($1.23 per book for California residents only).

Mail order form to: Insider Publications, 2124 Kittredge Street, Third Floor. Berkeley, CA 94704 USA. Or email to: info@travelinsider.com.

ORDER FORM
FOR THE WORLDWIDE GUIDE TO CHEAP AIRFARES

NAME

ADDRESS

CITY, STATE, POSTAL CODE, COUNTRY

TELEPHONE

PAYMENT METHOD (CIRCLE ONE)
CHECK   MONEY ORDER   VISA   MASTERCARD   AMEX

CREDIT CARD NUMBER, EXPIRATION DATE

NAME AS IT APPEARS ON THE CREDIT CARD

SIGNATURE OF CARDHOLDER

Please send me:

Book(s) @ $14.95 each = $

Shipping ($2.50 for the first book, $1 for each additional book)

Tax ($1.23 per book for California residents only)

                                              TOTAL $

Credit card orders will be shipped within 24 hours.